A PERSON
OF PAKISTANI
ORIGINS

A PERSON OF PAKISTANI ORIGINS

ZIAUDDIN SARDAR

HURST & COMPANY, LONDON

First published in the United Kingdom in 2018 by
C. Hurst & Co. (Publishers) Ltd.,
41 Great Russell Street, London, WC1B 3PL
© Ziauddin Sardar, 2018
All rights reserved.
Printed in the United Kingdom

Distributed in the United States, Canada and Latin America by
Oxford University Press, 198 Madison Avenue, New York, NY 10016,
United States of America

The right of Ziauddin Sardar to be identified as the author of this
publication is asserted by him in accordance with the Copyright, Designs
and Patents Act, 1988.

A Cataloguing-in-Publication data record for this book
is available from the British Library.

ISBN: 9781849049870

This book is printed using paper from registered sustainable
and managed sources.

www.hurstpublishers.com

CONTENTS

EXEMPTED FROM VISA
FOR ENTERING PAKISTAN -
AND POLICE REGISTRATION
AS OF PAKISTAN ORIGIN

M. YOUSAF ALI
COUNSELLOR
PAKISTAN HIGH COMMISSION
LONDON

DRAMATIS PERSONAE

Auntie Rashida, everyone's neighbourhood Auntie.

Dilip Kumar, leading Indian film actor and screenwriter.

Ehsan Danish, eminent Urdu poet noted for his revolutionary verse and known as 'Poet of the Workmen'.

Farid Mamu (Farid Ahmad Khan), my uncle, elder brother of my mother.

Gudu (Hameed Ahmad Khan), my cousin.

Guru Dutt, actor and director of classic Bollywood films.

Hafeez Jallundhri, celebrated Pakistani poet who wrote the national anthem.

Ibn Safi, prolific writer of detective novels.

Mahir al-Qadri, devout poet who wrote both religious and humorous verse.

Mumsey (Hamida Bagum), my mother.

Muqeet Mamu (Abdul Muqeet Khan), my uncle, younger brother of my mother-in-law.

Nana (Hakim Abdul Raiq Khan), brother of my grandfather and Grandfather of the entire extended family.

Nani Jan (Mukthari Bagum), my grandmother.

Waheed Mamu, my uncle, younger brother of my mother.

1.

••••••••

A PERSON
OF PAKISTANI
ORIGINS

••••••••

I

I don't know what came over me. Perhaps I could no longer live with the ambiguity. Perhaps the episodes of depressive illness precipitated by the very idea of getting yet another visa to visit my relatives in Pakistan had something to do with it. It culminated with the Pakistani cricket team. They began the 2017 International Cricket Council Champions Trophy as they always do: by losing to India. Then, something happened. They started winning, and in the final match of the tournament, they beat India. Correction: they clobbered India to become the Champions. I figured that something had changed not just with the Pakistani cricket team but with the country itself—and that, in turn, had changed something in me. The time had come for me to come out as 'A Person of Pakistani Origin'.

The odyssey had begun with a visit to see my friend Muneer Ahmad at the Pakistan High Commission in Knightsbridge. Ahmad, a genial, graceful man, has the official appellation 'First Secretary (Press)'. He has often gone out of his way to arrange visas not just for me but also for some of my journalist and writer friends—often at short notice. Could he, I asked, turn me into a bona fide person of Pakistani Origins? 'No problem,' he replied. 'I can arrange for you to get a NICOP or POC card. Then you can come and go without the need of a visa. I will make an appointment for you.'

A NICOP, or National Identity Card for Overseas Pakistanis, the High Commission website tells us, is for 'a Pakistani citizen living abroad or a dual nationality holder'. That's not me. I am

3

definitely not a Pakistani citizen—single or dual. POC, or Pakistani Origin Card, is for 'a foreigner with annulled Pakistani nationality or born to parents who have previously held Pakistani nationality'. That could be me. Both my parents 'held' Pakistani passports, and I too 'held' one, or rather a part of one, when I came to Britain on my mother's passport. I say could for a good reason. One could always be ambiguous and play with the idea that one is or is not a person of Pakistani origins. For me identity has always been malleable. There have been times when I have consciously chosen not to be a person of Pakistani origins, for example, when I worked in Saudi Arabia I insisted on being seen as British because it was the only way I could survive and overcome some of the Kingdom's racialised barriers. When the words 'origin' and 'Pakistan' are combined, they become problematic, and not just in the Arabian Peninsula, then or now. Are my origins located in the place I was born or can they be traced back in history to the religion, culture and civilisation I identify with? Jews, for example, trace their origins to ancient history, to the Prophet Abraham and the Fertile Crescent. Why should my origins be limited to a mere seventy years and a vaguely samosa shaped area on the world map? And was my place of birth always Pakistan, where history begins in 1947? Or is my birth place subcontinental, part of a bigger entity, a society with a long history that embraces all of India and all who settled in her over the centuries where the civilisation of Islam was moulded and flourished as an essential part of that complex whole? While such questions whirled in my mind, I had decided to put them aside. I am going, finally, to embrace my roots.

Apart from the usual forms and photographs, the application requires one to submit a host of documents that prove one's Pakistani origins: applicant's parents' Pakistani passports, parents' or spouse's National Identity Cards, birth certificate, marriage certificate, National Identity Cards of blood relatives in Pakistan, as well as a permanent address in Pakistan. I rummaged through boxes that my late father had carefully stored in the attic to find whatever documents I could. Armed with the relevant passports, ID cards and photocopies, I went, at an appointed time in December 2015, to the NADRA (National Database and Registration Authority) counter at the High Commission.

It did not go well. I returned home and penned an email to the High Commissioner:

> Sir—Yesterday I went to the High Commission to organise a POC card for myself and my wife. I thought that I should share my experience with you as it reflects very badly on how the High Commission treats the community.
>
> My appointment was at 3.00pm, kindly organised by Muneer Ahmad Sahib, Press Secretary. I went to the NADRA counter at the appointed time with Mr Nassir, who works in Ahmad Sahib's office. The person at the 'scrutiny' counter was exceptionally rude to Mr Nasser and asked me, in a rather off-handed fashion, to wait. I did not mind this as I could see there were many other people waiting before me. Indeed, there was a scrum towards the counter.
>
> I waited for about fifty minutes which provided me with an opportunity to observe what was going on. And I was upset with what I saw. The person at the counter was persistently rude to all. A young woman, holding a baby, was summarily dismissed from the counter, her questions unanswered. She left in tears, obviously distraught. Another young woman who had received an e-mail on her mobile was asked to give a print out; when she inquired how she could print from her iPhone she was shooed aside. She left shouting 'how rude'. I met a teacher from Southend who had taken a day off from school to get his NADRA card extended. He told me it was his third visit. His appointment was at 3.20pm. When he inquired about his turn he was told he did not have an appointment—despite the fact that he was holding a print out of an e-mail from the High Commission giving the details of his appointment. Again and again, people were being treated with indignity and disrespect in front of my eyes. The

5

two chaps at the counter seem to think that they were doing a favour to people who had come for their various cards rather than doing their job.

From where I was standing, I could clearly see inside the room where the fortunate few were ushered after their documents had been checked at the counter. It was in a state of total chaos. No one seemed to know what was going on. People were standing with their documents in their hands asking anyone they thought could help with the procedure—where, what, why were the constant refrains. No one had any idea what fee was required for what card. People were coming out agitated: they were asked to pay cash which they did not have with them and were desperately looking for an ATM machine.

When after fifty minutes, I inquired about my turn, one of the counter persons grudgingly asked for my documents. It seems that an appointment for my wife was not made, and only I could get my documents scrutinised. But by this time I had enough: I did not want to have anything to do with a High Commission that treats the British Pakistani community in such a disparaging and disgraceful manner, and seems so inept at doing something that is basically a bread and butter issue for the Embassy. I told him to forget it and left.

Yours sincerely, etc.

II

I left Pakistan at the age of ten, when my parents migrated to London. But ever since, Pakistan has refused to leave me. Believe me, there have been times when I have tried to ditch every last vestige of my Pakistani Self. When, for example, Pakistanis or persons of Pakistani origins are involved in terrorism. Alas, all too frequently. When, to give another example, the disturbing cases of 'sexual grooming' in Britain came to light. From June 2009 to May 2013, eight different groups of British Pakistani men, from Oldham, Rotherham, Derby, Nelson, Telford, Rochdale, and Oxford, were convicted of wholesale systematic abuse of young white girls. How could one possibly identify with such malevolence?

There have also been times when I positively wanted to stand up as a (British) Pakistani. In August 2011, three Pakistanis were killed in a hit-and-run incident in Birmingham: Haroon Jahan, Shazad Ali and Abdul Musavir Tariq. The incident is beautifully described in 'Birmingham for Tariq Jahan', a poem by Carol Ann Duffy:

> *After the evening prayers at the mosque,*
> *came the looters in masks,*
> *and you three stood,*
> *beloved in your neighbourhood,*
> *brave, bright, brothers,*
> *to be who you were—*
> *a hafiz is one who has memorised*
> *the entire Koran;*
> *a devout man—*
> *then the man in the speeding car*
> *who purposefully mounted the kerb ...*
> *I think we all should kneel*
> *on that English street,*
> *where he widowed your pregnant wife, Shazad,*
> *tossed your soul to the air, Abdul,*
> *and brought your father, Haroon, to his knees,*
> *his face masked in only your blood*
> *on the rolling news*
> *where nobody's children riot and burn.*

When it became clear that the culprits were Afro-Caribbean youths, riots broke out in the city. In an atmosphere of rising tension, with the police fearing revenge attacks and killings, Haroon Jehan's father, Tariq Jehan, diffused the situation with a few impromptu words of immense dignity: 'Why do we have to kill one another? Why are we doing this? I have lost my son. Step forward if you want to lose your sons. Otherwise, calm down and go home—please.' Revenge, said Jahan, was not what his faith and culture were all about. I was deeply moved and impressed by the immense composure of Jehan. I identified with his humanity, and through him with all of Pakistan.

There have even been times when the Pakistani segments of my complex Self have exploded in spontaneous joy. When, for example, Malala Yousafzai, who was shot by the Taliban, won the Nobel Prize for her efforts to promote female education in Pakistan. Or when I saw two Pakistani writers—Mohsin Hamid and Kamila Shamsie—on the Booker Prize long list. Unfortunately, such moments are relatively few.

Here is my dilemma. When I want nothing to do with Pakistan, it clings on to me. When I want to get close to Pakistan, it repels me; just as often, I am repelled by it. So there is a perpetual tug of war constantly pulling in opposite directions. I have been trying to resolve this quandary for decades, with little success.

In the early 1990s, I had also decided to embrace Pakistan as fully as I could. 'Pakistan,' I said, 'is an integral part of myself. I am going to do whatever I can for the land of my birth.' And what I was going to do was to organise a conference in Islamabad. Not just any conference. But one that would envision and develop some sort of plan to shape a better Pakistan in the not-too-distant future: a Pakistan one could cuddle with pride. I managed to persuade the World Futures Studies Federation (WFSF), on whose Executive Committee I served, to sponsor the conference and managed to raise a substantial sum from UNESCO for the event. I chased and convinced a number of prominent scholars and futurists from Pakistani diaspora communities, as well as from India, Bangladesh, Sri Lanka and Nepal to attend. The conference was to be held in Islamabad in July 1992.

We found a local host to look after the logistical arrangements, including visas and travel, and organise the programme.

A PERSON OF PAKISTANI ORIGINS

He was the founder and chair of the 'Pakistan Futuristic Institute', a small organisation devoted to exploring futures for Pakistan and came with high recommendations. So, without much hesitation, we bestowed on him the title of 'the Convenor'. Now, this is a true, story but I am going to follow the convention introduced by *Fargo*. At the beginning of every episode of the FX's black comedy and crime drama, we are told: 'at the request of the survivors, the names have been changed. Out of respect for the dead, the rest has been told exactly as it occurred'. So let's call our local host and Convenor 'Dr' Akram Azam. All the funding we had raised for the Conference was transferred to Dr Akram with recommendations on how the programme for the three-day event should be structured.

Meanwhile, I had to sort out my own visa. Up to that time I was getting a single entry 'family visa' that allows you to stay for up to ninety days. So every trip required a new visa, which meant early morning visits to the Pakistan High Commission, filling long forms, making sure you had the visa fee in the exact amount in cash—which could only be deposited in a branch of the Habib Bank located a mile from the High Commission—returning to join long, chaotic queues for hours to submit the paperwork, and other equally irritating and unsavoury undertakings. As I had decided to visit Pakistan regularly and frequently, I figured I should have a more permanent arrangement. It just so happened that an official at the High Commission at the time was some-how related to me. I say somehow because neither he nor I were actually sure what the relationship was. But there was a relation-ship: my best guess was that he was the son of a neighbour of one of my father's distant cousins. It is all I needed to persuade him to organise a more amenable visa regime for me. He came up trumps. I had special treatment. The stamp on my passport said: 'EXEMPTED FROM VISA FOR ENTERING PAKISTAN AND POLICE REGISTRATION...' I could visit Pakistan as frequently and as often as I wanted.

A PERSON OF PAKISTANI ORIGINS

Within days I was checking in at the Islamabad Hotel. I was eager to meet all the scholars from South Asia we had invited. But apart from Jim Dator, Professor of Political Science at the University of Hawaii and President of WFSF, there was no one there from outside Pakistan. Everyone I met was somehow related to Dr Akram. The Indian scholars, I was told, were denied visas. On the subcontinent Partition means Partition and never the twain shall meet. It is depressing, dispiriting and downright counterproductive, yet it endures. What is not yet amenable to change must be borne. Dr Akram had not bothered to organise travel for participants from Bangladesh, Sri Lanka and Nepal. Instead, he had spent the Conference funds on buying suitable gifts for the participants. With some pride, he handed me a handsome but rather heavy leather briefcase. Inside, there was a fetching shawl, a beautiful onyx box, a marble soap dish, a cotton shirt, a book of Dr Akram's self-published poetry. 'All made in Pakistan', Dr Akram informed me. I would have preferred a good cricket bat and equipment. But I suppressed my anger and said nothing.

The Conference began with high expectations. The opening ceremony was scheduled from 9.00 to 10.00am with speeches by dignitaries. I was slated to give the keynote address at 10.00. I sat amongst the audience listening to a high-ranking minister who extolled the virtues of the democratically elected government of Prime Minister Nawaz Sharif, then serving the first of his three terms. He was followed by another high-ranking minister singing the praises of Nawaz Sharif. And another. The audience became agitated and I sympathised with them. Then came a string of lower ranking ministers, one after another, all spoke a lot but said nothing. By 12 noon the Conference hall at the Islamabad Hotel was steaming with anger and frustration. When the junior ministers had finished, Dr Akram and his family members came to the podium to give endless votes of thanks. It was way past 1.00pm when the Chair invited me to come and give my 'address'.

I walked calmly to the podium. I looked at the Chair, turned to the audience, and said: 'My address is 9 Hillsea Street, London E1, United Kingdom.' I left the podium and returned to sit with the audience. Pandemonium broke out. The Chair insisted that I return to the podium and give a 'proper address'. I refused. The audience started shouting 'Speech! Speech'. I stood amongst the audience, and addressed the podium, which was still graced by a number of dignitaries. I described the future of Pakistan as a Greek tragedy: destined for disaster after disaster because of the moral ineptitude of its body politic. Even the good, innocent and wholesome in the country will turn toxic thanks to the intrinsic corruption of the elite. When I finished, I swiftly walked out of the Conference hall and went straight to my room.

I could not have been in my room for more than ten minutes when there was a knock at the door. I opened the door to two moustachioed men in *shalwar kameez*. They pushed their way in. 'Can we see your passport?' they demanded. I took out my passport and handed it to one of them. He flicked through the pages, and found the one with the EXEMPTED stamp. He looked at it for a moment, pulled a blue felt tip pen from his top pocket, and scribbled CANCELLED on the page. After handing the passport back, he said: 'You have 24 hours to leave Pakistan.'

Years would pass before I would return. Family ties, Catholic-like guilt for not doing something (anything) for Pakistan no matter how hard I tried to suppress all such feelings, and the odd conference or a book festival, made it necessary to return. Sometimes I felt like the beloved moth of Urdu poetry, constantly attracted to the flame, hurling itself towards a foregone conclusion. Other times, I would pinch myself, and mumble: what a cliché. Every visit to the land of the pure where hardly anything can be said to be uncontaminated was a test of my limited capacity for patience. I would return murmuring yet another pledge never to return to the place of my origins.

III

When we talk about 'Pakistani origins', what Pakistan are we talking about? It would be a cliché to say Pakistan is not a mono-lithic entity. There are several Pakistans. The Pakistan of the globalised rich, who move between Lahore and London, or Karachi and New York, is radically different from the Pakistan of the urban or rural poor whose only desire is to move out of their abject poverty. The Pakistan of the fanatic and uncouth Mullah, hell-bent on creating a *Shariah*-complaint state, could not be further removed from the Pakistan of the urbane, liberal elite. These are not just different 'readings' of Pakistan but distinc-tively different perceptions of what Pakistan is, should, and ought to be.

I am constantly juggling three different Pakistans. A Pakistan that is projected onto me by the perception of others; it does not matter where I go, it is always there. A Pakistan that is bigger than the geographical Pakistan; it incorporates the whole of South Asia, its long history and rich and diverse cultures. And a Pakistan of my memories.

After my parents moved to East London, it did not take long for me to realise that, whether I acknowledged my Pakistani origins or not, Pakistan would always be projected onto me. That my Pakistani origins were a problem for others became obvious when I started secondary school. During the late 1960s and early 1970s, a wave of racist violence was directed against the Asian community in Britain. Gangs of 'skinheads', as they were called, would roam the streets and single out people to attack. The press dubbed it 'Paki-Bashing'. I encountered skinheads regularly on the short walk from home to school. While the victims were predominantly Asians and Blacks, they are uniformly described as 'Pakistani', and often reported in the press as though they themselves, the victims, were responsible for initiating the violence. For example, on 26 April 1970, a grocery shop owned by a Pakistani was attacked by a group of skinheads. *The Times* described it as 'Pakistanis in clash', while the more liberal *Guardian* suggested it was 'three Pakistanis...in a fight with a group of skinheads'.

Even Pakistani dress was problematic. In December 1969, the headmaster of Kings Hill Primary School, Wednesbury, Staffordshire, one Harold Harvey, banned five Pakistani girls attending the school from wearing *shalwars*! It became a headline story. In those days, I used to edit *Zenith*, 'a monthly magazine for and by Muslim youth in Britain', that I had established. So I went to Wednesbury to get the girls' side of the story. The girls (Wikoran Nisa Kabir, 10; Naseema Patel, 8; Sakina Ahmad Patel, 7; and two sisters, Sheena Akhtar, 9 and Tanzeen Akhtar, 7) really liked their school and were clearly shocked at what happened. 'Mr Harvey came and said: "You can't come to school wearing baggy pants,"' Naseema Patel told me. Sakeena was forced to take her shalwar off. Naseema was told, 'go to your classroom and take your trousers off'. She refused and was sent home. When forced to give reasons for the ban, the headmaster said he was acting on the advice of the school nurse who had discovered the girls wearing shalwars 'were a little too dirty'. And the shalwar was interfering with the girls' physical education. The girls stayed home for four months during which time a pitched battle was fought between the school, supported by the local education authority, the parents and the Wednesbury Muslim Welfare Association. The school caved in just before the whole affair was about to go to court.

Pakistan, it seemed to me, was a dumping ground for all things malevolent in the psychological scaffolding of certain segments of British society. I can't recall reading a good story about Pakistan or Pakistanis, who only appeared in the news as criminals and racketeers. Even the people who should know better, and who one looked up to, had unsavoury views of Pakistan. Consider the case of Ian Botham who was knighted in 2007 for 'services to charity and to cricket'. He was a star player in England's 1983/84 tour of New Zealand and Pakistan. It was one of the worst tours in England's cricket history: they were beaten in the Test series both in New Zealand and Pakistan, lost three players through injury and certain members of the team were accused by *The Mail on Sunday* of smoking pot. In Pakistan, England's batsmen were confounded by the leg-breaks and googlies of Abdul Qadir. Botham had to return early from Pakistan for knee surgery. So when he was asked what he thought of Pakistan, what did Botham say? Given the woes and disasters of the team, and the fact that he was injured, he hardly had time to look at Pakistan. By all accounts, he hardly left the Hilton Hotel in Lahore where the team was staying. Pakistan is 'the kind of place', Botham said in a radio interview, 'to send your mother-in-law for a month, all expenses paid'. Not surprisingly, I, along with all of Pakistan, was rather upset.

So Botham found Pakistan to be a horrendous place. What was he comparing Lahore and Karachi with?

I got an opportunity to find out. A day or two after Botham made his comment, I was approached by the *Daily Express*. Would I go to Botham's hometown and see how it compares with Pakistan? Yes I would. Can you find out if it is the sort of place one would send one's mother-in-law for a holiday? Yes I can. So off I went to Scunthorpe, a place I had never heard of before but which, during the mid-1980s, had the highest concentration of Pakistanis outside Pakistan. My feature on the 'industrial garden town' appeared in the Wednesday 28 March 1984 edition of *Daily Express*, complete with a photo of me in front of the 'welcome to Scunthorpe' sign. It carried the title 'Curry on Scunthorpe', and the following strapline: 'After that bouncer, a Pakistani writer bowls along to inspect the state of play in Botham's home town'. Here's an extract:

> The situation became critical around 5.30 pm. I arrived in Scunthorpe just after 2pm on Saturday and checked into the Royal Hotel. The Royal is one of the two hotels in town. It has two stars to its credit. It offers a special reduction on weekends when, instead of the normal £31.00 one can secure a single room for almost half the price. The rooms come complete with a chipboard wardrobe, two MFI chairs, a dripping tap and toilet roll that refuses to settle down in its holder. You also get a 'Royal Breakfast', a close second to British Rail's 'traveller's fare,' and a free copy of the glossy *Humberside and South Yorkshire Executive*.

> Saving the *Executive* for my bedtime reading, I ventured out to savour Scunthorpe's gastronomic delights.

> I found a number of restaurants in the High Street and around Doncaster Road. They were all closed. I walked up the High Street, through the red brick shopping centre to the cultural heart of the town. At Scunthorpe Civic Theatre 'No Man's Land' was in production. The nearby Scunthorpe Film Theatre was showing *Grease 2*. My feelings exactly.

> There was still nowhere to eat. I walked all the way back and crossed over to Doncaster Street. It was almost 5 o'clock and my intestines were begging for mercy. I decided to settle for a bag of fish and chips and popped over to the 'Hungry Fisherman'.

> I was quite glad to hand over my 99p. 'That's how they do things in Scunthorpe,' I said. 'Let me eat like a native'. But a few bites later I encountered some unexpected protein, in the shape of a long, curly, blonde hair, which I am sure, had received a generous supply of Harmony Hairspray that morning.

> I had to fall back on a curry from Hamida's take away in Frodingham Road.

A PERSON OF PAKISTANI ORIGINS

Fish and chips, in fact, are Scunthorpe's second major industry. It was in a fish and chip shop, just like 'The Hungry Fisherman', that a certain Mr Riley, a local man, first discovered the crisp. Since then, 'Riley's crisps' have gone down in history. And the local crisp industry is the biggest employer of Scunthorpe's women.

But the backbone of Scunthorpe industry is steel. From the Stone Age till the arrival of steel, the local council handbook openly admits, the history of the town is largely 'uneventful'. Steel arrived in Scunthorpe in 1880. By the early twentieth century, the steel industry provided full employment for Scunthorpe. It also stamped its personality on the town.

'Steel is a seven-day industry', explained a local Councillor. 'Steel workers work every day, including Sunday. Steel mills operate 24 hours. So at any given time, half the town is sleeping, while the other half is working.'

He went on: 'Sunday is no different than any other day for us. Comedians who do not understand the steel industry have made Scunthorpe into a music-hall joke. 'As dead as Scunthorpe on Sunday' is a line I have heard often.' He was bitter that comedians 'take the micky out of Scunthorpe.' 'There is no such thing as the Scunthorpe Symphony Orchestra,' he says. 'There never has been. These people never talk about our achievements.'

'Such as?' I ask eagerly.

'Well, we are in the *Guinness Book of Records* for making the longest sausage in the world,' he says triumphantly.

'What does one do on a Saturday night in Scunthorpe?' I ask, changing the subject.

'Well, there's lots of pubs. And working men's clubs. You can drink there.'

'And what if you do not drink?'

'Ah, I sympathise with you Pakistanis who do not drink. There is plenty of air in Scunthorpe. They can go for a walk and breathe fresh air.'

A PERSON OF PAKISTANI ORIGINS

I say goodbye to my Councillor friend and visit the Ashdown Club, where I am signed in by Fred Kirk, a rugged man in his middle-age, who says his working men's club boasts the Bar Maid of the Year. He gives me a slip marked 'CAUTION'. I read: 'visitors are *strictly prohibited* from purchasing, or attempting to purchase, directly or indirectly, any *excisable articles* while visiting the Club.'

Inside, a number of old and not-so-old couples sit in three straight rows. In an adjacent room a group of rowdy men shoot pool. An older looking gentleman is seriously occupied with a slot machine. Two younger men seemed to be hypnotised by 'Warlords'. They press buttons and kick the machine simultaneously. Through the beer fumes and cigarette smoke I can make out a group of musicians at the end of the hall competing for attention. A sticker on the wall tells me 'Nightshift' are playing.

I speak to a group of club enthusiasts. 'Nice place.' I force my words. 'Yeh,' replies an old man. 'You should have been here on New Year's Day,' says a younger woman sitting next to him. 'I am Kath Smith,' she introduces herself. 'We had men and women wrestling. Big Mama versus Geordie Kay. That's her,' she points towards a large, busty woman. 'And you know what,' she taps me on the shoulder and continues, 'Jean Collins and Maureen Clixby—that's them over there—took Keith Blentchere's pants off. He's our concert secretary. I took a photograph. Do you want to see it?'

Time to move on I say to myself. 'Where would you go for an evening out, apart from coming to the Club,' I ask Kath.

'Well, there's Garbos in the High Street. And, of course, Scene 3.' I take down the addresses and say a fond farewell to Kath.

Outside, it was pitch dark and raining. I arrived at Garbos just after ten. I knocked on the door and two seven foot bouncers pulled me in. It was pretty posh inside. The seats around the bar were mainly occupied by middle aged men who had placed themselves strategically. Near the dance area, all the women sat on one side of the hall talking among themselves. All the men stood against the opposite wall, beer glasses in hand, looking lost. Every now and again someone would walk straight into the huge mirror covering an entire wall and making the hall look twice its size. A rather large woman danced with herself and occupied most of the dancing floor, I admired her courage. A couple of young girls made a fresh appearance. Two young men rushed to ravish these beauties, or at least would have ravished them, if the girls had not pre-empted them by timely compliance.

Over at Scene 3, there was a queue to get in. I got past the bouncers while they were taking care of a disoriented skinhead. I moved around. I was greeted by flashing lights and throbbing Scunthorpe thighs. Three television screens were flashing the message: 'Congratulations Ann and John on your wedding anniversary and also Ann's birthday.'

I moved to the 'Quiet room' where a number of couples were preying on each other, or at least it appeared as if fervent worshipful attentions were being exchanged. The 'Quiet room' led to the main dance area where the disc jockey was telling the crowd to 'move to 'Relax', the number one hit from Frankie Goes to Hollywood'. He pushed the single onto his record player and started to play with his Commodore Vic 20 personal computer. Flashing lights began to change colour and a psychedelic image appeared on a large screen. The crowd on the dance floor began to swing in a somewhat unco-ordinated and violent manner, with some individuals not so much dancing but doing funny walks.

Back at the Ashdown Club folk were not much impressed by Scene 3. 'Three quid to get in, quid for a lager. We haven't got that sort of money,' says an unemployed steel worker. 'As dead as Scunthorpe on Sunday, you say. This town's dead every day, mate. It's just dead. The only thing this town has going for it mate is that its next to the M18. One minute to the motorway and you are out.'

That's fine if you're driving. But if you are taking the train it is not so easy to get out of Scunthorpe. On arrival at the station, at around two o'clock on Sunday, I discovered there were no trains. 'It's the bus to Doncaster luv,' said the cheerful station clerk. And there was a full two hours wait for the next one.

A PERSON OF PAKISTANI ORIGINS

I admired the grey architecture of Scunthorpe Station and thought of Faisalabad Junction. At least if offers a greater variety of colour, smell and foodstuff. You have no chance of getting bored or hungry. 'Are there any souvenirs I can take back from Scunthorpe', I ask a fellow passenger waiting for the bus.

'Not really,' he says. And after a pause he adds with a grin, 'Well there's Doreen. She could give you a thing or two to take back.'

Over the last few decades, I have observed how anti-Pakistani sentiments, such as those expressed by Botham in an off-the-cuff remark, became widespread. For a while, they were limited to particular groups in certain countries such as Britain and the United States. But major events of our era, such as the Rushdie affair of the 1990s, the 11 September 2001 atrocity and the 7 July 2005 London bombings, provided major boosts and turned these sentiments into a full-blown global trend. Pakistan itself has played a major part in fuelling this resentment.

The shooting dead of the Governor of Punjab, Salman Taseer in January 2011, in Lahore, and the case of Aasia Bibi, both galvanised anti-Pakistani sentiment across the planet. Aasia Bibi, a labourer and mother of five from the Christian community, was accused of blasphemy and sentenced to death. Taseer was killed for defending her and his murderer hailed as a hero by certain sections of Pakistani society. It can be said that apart from Pakistani terrorists, the country's blasphemy laws are a major source of resentment against Pakistan. So now the very word 'Pakistan' comes wrapped in racialised sentiments. Immigration officers throughout the Western world can instantly spot a person of Pakistani origins. The *shalwar kameez* are always an obvious giveaway, yet you can't escape the wrath of immigration officers even if your name is Khan. In one specific instance, Shah Rukh Khan, from India, a world famous Bollywood superstar clad in an Armani suit, was stopped and questioned. Such are the ways of racial profiling. The irony is that Shah Rukh

Khan's most singular contribution was to make the film *My Name Is Khan* whose plot concerns the determined efforts of a South Asian American to inform none other than President George W Bush of the simple truth: 'My name is Khan and I am not a terrorist.'

I tended to avoid specific countries in the aftermath of the horrors of 9/11. But in April 2002, I had to visit the United States to promote my book, *Why Do People Hate America?*, co-authored with my long-time collaborator, the anthropologist, television producer and writer, Merryl Wyn Davies. The book uses Hollywood movies to make its argument: America has appropriated the traditional arguments for God. Whereas these arguments were conventionally used to justify the existence of God, people around the world now see them as providing valida-tion for American behaviour. There are four such arguments. In the first, the cosmological argument for God, derived originally from Aristotle, God is described as the cause of everything. Instead of God, America has now become the cause of every-thing. The presence of the US is felt in every corner of the globe. Its foreign policies affect us all. Nothing seems to move without America's consent. The second, the ontological argu-ment for God's existence, attributed to St Anselm, goes some-thing like this: God is the most perfect being, it is more perfect to exist than not exist, therefore, God exists. Ontological argu-ments infer that something exists because certain concepts are related in certain ways. Good and evil are related as opposite. So if evil exists there must also be good. America relates to the world through such ontological logic: because 'terrorists' are evil, America is good and virtuous. The 'Axis of Evil' out there implicitly positions US as the 'Axis of Good'. But this is not simply a binary opposition: the ontological element, the nature of American being, makes America *only* Good and virtuous. It is a small step then to assume that you are chosen both by God and

History. How often have we heard American leaders proclaim that God is with them, or that History has called on America to act? The third argument is existential. Like God, America exists for, in and by itself. All global life must, willingly or unwillingly, pay total homage to the de facto existence of the US. For America, nothing matters except its own interests; the interests, needs, concerns, and desires of all nations, all people, indeed the planet itself, must be subservient to the interests of the US and the comfort and consumption of American lifestyle. The fourth and final argument is definitional. In religious thought, the power to define what is good and what is bad, what is virtue and what is not, lies solely in the hands of God. But in the contemporary world, America has become the defining power. America now defines what is 'free market', 'international law', 'human rights' and 'freedom of the press'—and who is a 'fundamentalist', 'terrorist', or simply 'evil'. The rest of the world, including Europe, must accept these definitions and follow the American lead. Promoting a book with these arguments in 'The Land of the Free' was going to be tad hazardous.

A number of major American publishers first accepted the book and then pulled out. It was finally published by a small, newly formed company named with whimsical irony— Disinformation Books. Its list consisted of current affairs titles exposing conspiracy theories, political scandals and corporate fraud. The company's best known title was *Everything You Know Is Wrong: The Disinformation Guide to Secrets and Lies* by the editor and investigative journalist Russ Kick. The company had organised a promotion tour in New York and Washington. I was rather reluctant, but Disinformation's CEO, Gary Baddeley, who happened to be British, came over from New York to reassure me. 'Don't worry,' he said. 'I will be with you all the way.'

We flew from London to New York together. Just before we landed, Baddeley tapped me on the shoulder and said: 'Do not mention, under any circumstances, that you are here to promote *Why Do People Hate America?* At JFK airport, Baddeley led the way and presented mine and his (British) passports together to the Immigration officer. The officer examined his passport, scanned it, and stamped it, and then handed it back to him. 'Welcome to America,' he said. Then he examined my passport carefully. He looked up at me, and was about to stamp my passport when he stopped in mid-motion. 'You were born in Dipalpur,' he said. 'Where is that?' 'It is the part of Pakistan that is located in East London,' I replied. 'In that case, Sir, you have to take a little detour.'

The officer asked Baddeley, who was standing beside me, to move on. He raised his hand and waved it in the direction of a group of immigration officials who were standing at one end of the arrival hall observing the proceedings. One of them ran over to our counter. The immigration officer placed my passport in a small cellophane bag and handed it to him. 'Sir, please go with him.'

I was taken to large room. On one side of the room, there was a raised platform with a huge table, behind which sat three rather stern looking officers. Their haircut and general demeanour, I surmised derived from a shared military background. The rest of the room was filled with anxious looking people of Chinese and Latin American origins. My passport was passed on to the first officer and I was asked to sit down.

I sat patiently in front of the officer for about three hours. I could clearly see my passport, wrapped in the cellophane bag, on his table next to a pile of other passports. He was going through them one by one. Every now and then, he would call someone over and question them. It was obvious from the process, and the accumulated pile of passports amassed besides him, that it would take many hours before he would get to mine. I also noted that virtually all the cases he was dealing with involved people migrating to the US. So I approached him and said: 'Sir, I am only a visitor. You can get rid of me quickly. I will be happy to be deported.' The officer picked up my passport, flicked through its pages, and said: 'OK. Take a seat.'

I returned to my chair. The officer checked things on his computer terminal for several minutes. Then he left his post and disappeared for a few minutes. He returned with a huge pile of photocopies, which he placed neatly by his terminal. Then he began what looked like a systematic military operation: he would pick a photocopy from one pile, look at it carefully, then look at the photo in my passport, then put the photocopy in a second pile. I realised he was physically comparing my photo with photos on a suspect list. This pile was even bigger than the pile of the passports he had previously been wading through. It would take, I estimated, a day or so for him to complete his careful scrutiny.

I lost the residue of my miniscule quotient of patience. 'Sir,' I said approaching his desk, 'you don't have to do this. My face is well known. I am a famous writer.'

The officer stared at me for a few moments. 'Yeh', he said. 'How famous?'

'Reasonably famous.'

'If I put your name in a search engine, how many hits would I get?'

'I don't know', I replied. 'Maybe 100,000. Or even a quarter of a million'.

He typed my name in Yahoo, and pressed the return key. I do not know how many hits there were but the first one was *Why Do People Hate America?*

Suddenly, the official became rather animated. 'Aah. You are the author of this book?'

I nodded my head.

'I know why people dislike us,' he said. Then he leaned forward as though he was whispering to me. 'Originally from Pakistan?'

'Yes,' I mumbled.

'And you are here to promote your book.'

I nodded my head, again.

'Why didn't you say so.' He stamped my passport and handed it back to me. 'Welcome to America,' he said.

IV

Pakistanis have a strange love/hate relationship with America. At any given time, half the population cannot wait to leave the country and migrate to 'Amerika'. The remaining half relies on American aid without which the country is always on the verge of economic collapse. Yet, most Pakistanis blame the US for most of their problems. There is the 'war on terror', and the associated 'drone strikes', that have ravaged the country. As an ally of Pakistan, the US is like a scorpion: it is in its nature to sting. The miracle is that Pakistan has survived despite being stung numerous times; the irony is that it insists on being stung again and again. However paranoid Pakistan may be about America (and looking for conspiracies is a favourite national pastime), the real problems of Pakistan are much closer to home.

Home. That's the problem. Or rather the absence of home. The territorial state called 'Pakistan' does not serve as a home to the entirety of its heterogeneous, multifaceted population. Basically, Pakistan is an amalgam of three city states: Karachi, Lahore and Islamabad/Rawalpindi. Each one has its own distinct identity and ways of doing things, and there is quite a rivalry between them. A home is a place of consolation and community, security and sensibility, warmth and tenderness, as well as lineage and familial values. It is seldom that one comes across a Pakistani who feels 'at home' in Pakistan: that is, someone who feels safe and secure—politically, economically, and psychologically, sees the possibility of positive change, and takes it for granted that their past, present and future belong to and in Pakistan. As such, there is no self-belief in Pakistan, about Pakistan or indeed in being a person of Pakistani origins.

The Pakistani Self is a truncated Self, a false Self, an aimless *awara* Self that can never find solace and comfort of home in the physical and mental territory within which it is located. It is a curtailed Self because it has cut itself off from the culture and imagination of the region to which it belongs. Pakistan is the product of Partition. Partition is a product of the colonial mind-set that was self-inflicted upon a beguiled body of opinion as the panacea to purge all the ills of colonialism and its history. Partition was a traumatic rupture that has left painful scar tissue that still suppurates and spurts poison. Turned out from its natural ancestral home, Pakistan looks to Saudi Arabia for inspiration, yet—apart from an arid notion of religion—it has no affinity with the desert Kingdom. It suppresses or shuns the history and culture of which it is an integral part—the ethos not just of subcontinental Islam, but also the beauty of Bharatanatyam and Kathakali, the contentment of Yoga and the brilliance of Jain metaphysics, Hindu philosophy and the paths of Buddhism, Dilip Kumar, Guru Dutt and classical Bollywood, and the poetic genius of all the Urdu poets from Amir Khusro and Vali Daccani to Josh and Faiz. The Pakistani Self is distorted because it is divorced from the South Asian imagination, the kaleidoscope of 'Hindustan'. This is why Pakistani culture suffers from a deep inferiority complex.

It is a false Self because it is based on lies and distortions of history. In his *The Murder of History*, a forensic examination of history textbooks in Pakistan, K. K. Aziz shows that the history that Pakistanis are fed, and ultimately believe, is nothing but cheap propaganda. He identifies four messages that history books promote: follow the dictates of the regime in power, support military rule, glorify wars and hate India. These messages are produced by fabricating an anti-colonial past; tracing every political, social, intellectual, religious and intellectual development that took place in Muslim India to the Aligarh movement and the United Provinces; creating and imposing a new culture on Pakistan; and simply by fabrication. Aziz suggest that these falsehoods have led to the ruin of Pakistan. Since Pakistanis lie about their own history, about themselves, they are unable to see anything within Pakistan as true and authentic.

I had not realised how much I too, a diasporic person in search of my Pakistani origins, suffer this sense of separation and loss. It was Merryl Wyn Davies who pointedly reminded me how the truth burst forth. I am not a person noted for displaying sentiment. My metier runs more to sardonic wit, outright sarcasm and what I would term a puckish sense of humour—though I have heard it called malevolent. I find this mode operates for all circumstances and occasions—and yet...

In 1996, I was asked by my dear friend, the Indian intellectual and writer Ashis Nandy, to deliver the first Saadat Hassan Manto Lecture, which was to be held at the Nehru Memorial Museum and Library in Delhi. We had spent the best part of a month touring around India contemplating the possibilities of various projects to mark the 500th anniversary of the arrival in India of Vasco da Gama and hence the coming of colonialism. I had written my lecture before leaving London. Manto is a renowned short story writer and a particular hero of mine. Born in India, he removed to Pakistan and better than anyone else captures, conveys, analyses, understands, explores and portrays the complex inner selves of the subcontinent and the violence these selves have visited on their being. Most of all, Manto writes of Partition and its multi-layered consequences often in harrowing, emotionally draining, concise, and perfectly formed intriguing stories. I never read a lecture. It is my practice to present the audience with a riff, a series of vignettes of the ideas contained in the written version, enough to whet their appetite and send them off to the text with some key concepts in mind. So there I stood, warming to my subject, reprising some of the most salient insights and subtleties that Manto as a man of the Subcontinent, and example *par excellence* of the subcontinental imagination, had to offer. I began to draw some conclusions and as I did so I felt a strange sensation, a welling up. I spoke of how Manto's work made evident the truth of the natural belonging that subsists between all the cultures and identities of the subcontinent, of the unnatural brutality its people have practised on themselves by partitioning not only the land area but the mental space, the history, aesthetic and sensibility of their mutual belonging. 'It is the duty of our generation to reclaim the past and reunite our futures,' I heard myself saying in an increasingly quivering voice, as I became aware that tears were starting to course down my cheeks. This was more than unexpected. It was not just homage to Manto, it was evidence of the existence of a deep artesian well of meaning that could irrigate and fructify the regeneration and self-comprehension of the subcontinental imagination. I was there in Delhi and these words needed to be said. It was a close encounter with all the ambiguities of my being as a person of Pakistani Origin and it over whelmed me with the potency of its emotional truth.

Unanchored from history as well as the South Asian imagination, the Pakistani Self is aimless—*awara*, vagabond, homeless at home. As such it has no conception of collective responsibility or notion of a home that belongs to a diverse multitude. Its only source of comfort is power. Not surprisingly, every societal institution, whether it is the military or political dynasties, feudal landlords or the judiciary, pursues power solely for itself and seeks to entrench itself in power. With few exceptions, Pakistani politicians are feudalists who want to keep the landless peasants on their land uneducated and dependent. Political parties are structured on feudal patterns, and led by feudal leaders who run them as their private properties, passing on their inheritance to their children. If it is not the Nawaz household, it is the Bhutto ménage: the father, the daughter, the husband, and the half-wit, semi-literate son (yes, you can be semi-literate even if you have been to Oxford). The judiciary too is feudalist, and deeply hide-bound. The military is a law unto itself. Not content with being a business corporation, it insists on dabbling in politics and being at the centre of decision-making in almost every institution. Its presence can be felt everywhere and throughout all levels of soci-ety—from the fortified streets of the country's main cities to its 'defence colonies', in the universities and even in the national cricket team. Every major national institution has one or two retired or serving members of the army in its governing body. So every societal organisation has created its own power enclave, its own little exclusive 'home'.

A curtailed, deceptive, adrift Self is a Self that has lost its humanity. It cannot create an inclusive home. It transforms not just the past but also the present and the future into a foreign country, a state where no one is at home. Its energy is devoted exclusively to creating mini enclaves—defence colonies—that create demarcations between different segments of a diverse soci-ety. These borders are not just about an external expanse of land but also internal psychological spaces. The distorted Self that demarcates the boundaries also determines non-home at the same time: all those who do not belong, or are impure, or are powerless, must be kept away from home and banished. This is why all those who maintain that Pakistan was created for Islam insist that it was created only for their particular kind of Islam. Notice how various groups of Sunnis and Shias in Pakistan regard each other as strangers: at the very least one must be suspicious of the Other if one is not actively persecuting and killing them.

A PERSON OF PAKISTANI ORIGINS

The faith of others is always impure, polluted and dangerous and as such does not belong in their miniscule home. The minority Ahmadis are thus a threat to the country, its constitution and its ideology. The Christians and the Hindus are not pure enough for the land of the pure.

Indeed, the pure lack so much self-confidence that they have to insist on draconian blasphemy laws that serve both as an excuse and an instrument for the purification of their land. Defenceless women and children are framed and accused of blasphemy and then sentenced to death by a cowardly, shameless judiciary. The diminished Self, deprived of its humanity, cannot relate to others and hence has no sense of ethics or morality. This is why the Taliban can bomb a school and lynch mobs can beat a student to death for alleged blasphemy. The segregated Self can only produce segregation, bigotry, violence and mob rule. It has to be said: if Pakistan was born in the name of Islam then it is also being destroyed in the name of Islam.

For the segregated enclaves to survive, it is necessary for the status quo to be maintained. As such, neither the politicians, nor the feudal landlords, nor the army nor the judiciary, are interested in promoting education and social justice, economic progress, communal harmony or well-being. This is why the main concern of all parties is to hang on to their own segment of power by any means necessary. The consequence: the country is perpetually in paralysis. A paranoid media intensifies the worst aspects of the status quo—intolerance, jingoism and religious extremism.

A distorted, disturbed Self cannot express itself in rational and sane ways. It reveals itself only in extreme positions. Hence, the varieties of extremisms in Pakistan are truly dumbfounding. Even religious fundamentalism spans a wide spectrum. At one end we find the Taliban who have unleashed a tsunami of zealotry that has almost drowned Pakistan. At the other end, there is what we may call a 'gentle fundamentalism' best illustrated by the late pop star and fashion entrepreneur, Junaid Jamshed.

During the 1990s, Jamshed, who died tragically in a plane crash in December 2016, was a rock star in Pakistan. As the lead singer of 'Vital Signs', the band that laid the foundation for the country's thriving rock music industry, he was adored by young and old alike. The group was responsible for a string of commercial and critical hits, including the unofficial Pakistani anthem, 'Dil Dil Pakistan' ('My Heart is Pakistan'). He went on to have successful careers as a solo artist and television personality.

But in 2004, Jamshed found religion, or, as he put it, decided to devote his life to Islam. More specifically, he joined the Tablighi Jamaat, a fundamentalist religious movement. He denounced music, established a charity, and became a preacher. His sermons, widely available on YouTube, are a good illustration of one particular strand of fundamentalism deeply rooted in Pakistani soil. For Tablighi Jamaat Islam is all about ritual and supplication. Its brand of Islam is based on just six points: correct belief, regular prayer, praising God, sincerity of intention, respect for other Muslims and devoting time to preaching. All human problems, Tablighi Jamaat tells its followers, can be solved by prayer and proselytising. And that's exactly what Jamshed preached.

However, in the Tablighi framework, respect for other Muslims does not include respect for women. The Tablighis are aggressively misogynistic. Jamshed regularly berated women as inferior to men, and argued that they needed to be put in their place. Women need to be covered up, isolated, and told to shut up. But in November 2014, he went a bit too far. While explaining his views on the inherent inferiority of women, Jamshed related a story about Ayesha, the youngest wife of the Prophet Muhammad, and how she feigned an illness to gain the attention of her husband. The story, he concluded, 'proves that a woman cannot be reformed even if she is in the gathering of the Prophet'. That brought him into direct conflict with another equally popular variety of Pakistani fundamentalism.

It is best represented by the creepy television preacher Aamir Liqquat Hussain, a former politician and Minister of Religious Affairs. Hussain, who hands out orphaned children as prizes on his television show, goes out of his way to appear liberal and open minded. He has denounced violence, suicide bombing and gives lip service to Muslim unity. But he is a fundamentalist puritan. For him, the traditional sources and sacred personalities of Islam are above criticism. They have to be accepted, revered and obeyed without question. Not surprisingly, he saw Jamshed's swipe at Ayesha as disrespectful. The 'Disco Mullah' had committed an act of blasphemy, Hussain declared on one of his shows. Within a day, the Sunni Tehreek, a national grouping of clerics, had launched a sit-in in Karachi to demand Jamshed's arrest. A First Information Report (FIR) was registered against him, and the police sought his arrest. Jamshed escaped to his London pad from where he issued a grovelling apology.

Both Tablighi Jamaat and Sunni Tehreek represent a fundamentalism that is ingrained in traditionalism. But they are traditionalisms of different types; a difference that can be seen in their respective beards. The Tablighi beard is a thick, unruly affair, with shaved upper lip. The Prophet, they suggest, had a beard the length of a fist—which is what devout Muslims should have. It can be seen flowing on Jamshed as well as England cricket team all-rounder Moin Ali and the South African batsman, Hashim Amla—the most famous beard in contemporary Islam. In contrast, Sunni Tehreek argues that the Prophet had a well-kept beard that was sometimes coloured with henna. Their followers have shorter, groomed beards which on occasions may have a deep red tint. While Tablighis are obsessed with rituals, Sunni Tehreek is into adoration of saints.

Its hundreds of millions of followers regard the Prophet as a special kind of human being created from light who is always present at any time and any place, and venerate the household of the Prophet as well as dead and living saints. While Tablighi Jamaat regards politics as evil and argues that sincere Muslims should shun all politics, Sunni Tehreek is actively involved in politics—indeed, it has been in the forefront of the blasphemy movement. Its political wing, Jamiat Ulema-e-Pakistan (JUP), contests elections and vigorously promotes its brand of traditional, folk-based fundamentalism.

However, Sunni Tahreek's politics is radically different from another fundamentalist group, the Jamaat-e-Islami. Established in British India in 1941, Jamaat-e-Islami is an ideological movement with a strong authoritarian tendency. Its basic aim is to transform Pakistan into an 'Islamic state'. The late Abul ala Maududi, its founder and long-time leader, argued that Islam is a total system that regulates all aspect of human behaviour—social, economic, personal, psychological as well as political. As such, Islam and state are intrinsically linked. Islam is both: the religion of the state as well as the state itself. The state must be ruled by the *Shariah*, or Islamic law, and the best rulers could only be those who had knowledge and expertise in Islamic law and who are recognised by the populace as the true guardians of Islam: the *ulema* or the religious scholars.

While Jamaat-e-Islami has failed politically it has succeeded in spreading another brand of fundamentalism in Pakistan. It emerged during the decade (1978–88) when the military dictator General Zia ul-Haq was in power. Urged on by Saudi Arabia, and aided and encouraged by Jamaat-e-Islami, Zia ul-Haq sought to 'Islamise' Pakistan by introducing *Shariah* law, blasphemy ordinances, establishing madrassas and banning music and film. It was all an attempt to establish the Wahhabi doctrine, the Saudi brand of puritanical Islam, as the dominant sect of Pakistan. A product of the inferiority complex of Pakistani society's own understanding and interpretations of Islam, it turned out to be a successful venture.

I met General Zia ul-Haq in the winter of 1985. I was an advisor to a Saudi delegation that was visiting Pakistan. At the Presidential House in Islamabad, the General greeted us warmly. The delegation was treated to a long speech which involved lavish praise for the Afghan jihad, led by the young Osama bin Laden, and over 30,000 foreign jihadis who had come from 43 different countries to fight in Afghanistan. By popular demand, the General said, he was going to introduce the *Shariah, à la* Saudi Arabia, in Pakistan. He described in some detail how criminals would be lashed, thieves would have their hands cut off humanely, and adulterers would be stoned. Islam, the President announced, was a 'total system' and as such had to be 'imposed on society in its totality'.

At a dinner in honour of the delegation, I was asked to sit at the President's table. What happened next is described in my book *Desperately Seeking Paradise* in these words:

> During the first course—lentil soup—he again chatted with everyone about his passion for the Shariah. When the main course—biryani, lamb korma, and mixed vegetable—arrived, he suddenly turned towards me.

> 'Do I look like a deranged dictator to you?' he demanded. The whole table was stunned and immediately everyone seemed to find their food fascinating. I was conscious of turmoil in my inner self. Diplomacy is not my strong suit; tact, caution and a prudential turn of phrase have long been strangers to my nature. My instant reaction was to shout out: 'YES!' I wrestled spontaneity to a draw and merely sat still and quiet. There is a famous Latin epithet to the effect that silence is assent, this would have to do.

> President Zia-ul-Haq did not look angry. He seemed amused. 'In your book, *Islamic Futures*', he said beaming, 'you describe me as a deranged dictator'. He signalled to an aide to come forward. The

aide, in full military uniform, came running with a copy of the book, already opened at the relevant page.

The President read: 'No wonder that the average Muslim cringes with fear at the mention of "Islamic rule". And every time an attempt is made to turn a country into an "Islamic state", as in Pakistan, Libya, or in the Sudan, their worst fears are realised. The picture is always the same: a deranged dictator sits on the throne charged with the belief that he has a divine mandate to impose Islam on the masses. His first actions are to introduce "Islamic punishments"—as if Islam begins and ends with them—and various public floggings take place to convey the message that he means business. Various groups of ulema—religious scholars—and Islamic parties seek appointments in his government and applaud his actions. He declares women to be non-entities, establishes a "Council of Islamic Ideology" and various "Shariah courts" where summary justice is seen to be done. Can there be a better invitation to Islam than this?' He closed the book and chuckled. Everyone at the table joined in laughter, with a tinny edge of nervousness. But I wasn't sure whether they were laughing at me or the President. The conversation moved on to other topics.

Just before we left the Presidential House, I was presented with a gift: an exceptionally heavy table lamp made of solid green marble, packed in a wooden case, covered with red velvet. Once again, I would have preferred some cricket gear.

By the time the next military dictator, General Pervez Musharraf, came into power in 1999, intolerant Wahhabism had become the dominant creed in Pakistan. The jihadis, local and foreign, showered with praise by General Zia, were now showering bullets all over Pakistan. After the war against the Soviet Union, the jihadis joined Al-Qa'ida and the Taliban to fight against the US. Then they turned on Pakistan itself. The Taliban splintered into various factions such as Tahrik-e-Taliban Pakistan and Jammat-ul-Ahrar. During the late 1980s and the

1990s, four local militant outfits emerged—Sipha-e-Sahaba Pakistan (SAP), Lashkar-e-Jhangvi, Josh-e-Muhammad and Lashkar-e-Tayyaba. A decade later, they had splintered into over eighty 'Punjabi Talibans'—each as psychotic as the other. But toxic Islam was not limited to vicious groups and organisations. It spread first incrementally and then rapidly throughout the Pakistani society. Thanks to General Zia, a large segment of the Pakistani middle class, including the army, now subscribed to Wahhabi fundamentalism.

Wahhabism was a perfect fit for Pakistan's truncated Self. As an ahistorical ideology that abhors history, Wahhabism suited a state built on falsification and distortion of history.

As a puritan creed, Wahhabism anchored the aimless, *awara* Self: it served as a home away from home for the deep inferiority complex of Pakistani society. And Wahhabism's self-righteousness and insistence of imposing its notion of righteousness on others, justified the arrogance of those who could not deal with diversity and sought solace and comfort in naked power. It was manna from heaven for the self-proclaimed guardians of Pakistan's public morality. Intolerance, misogyny, xenophobia and inhumanity now had a religious justification.

General Musharraf came to power by overthrowing the democratic government of Prime Minister Nawaz Sharif. I came face to face with him in April 2005. I was in Pakistan filming what the BBC described as 'an epic journey through five Muslim countries'. Apart from Pakistan, my voyage took me to Indonesia, Malaysia, Morocco and Turkey—the periphery of the Muslim world that houses a majority of the world's Muslims. Part of the assignment for the 90-minute documentary was to interview the political leaders of each country. Thus an appointment was made for me to interview President Musharraf through the good offices of the BBC.

I went to 'Army House' in Rawalpindi to meet the General. We were searched, our mobiles confiscated, and our filming equipment unfrocked and extensively examined. Eventually, we were taken to the 'Sun Room', a large conservatory adjacent to the main building. It was tastefully decorated with Samurai swords, state-of the-art music and cinema equipment and fine Havana cigars. 'This is where the President comes to relax,' we were told. Before the interview started, General Sultan, the chief press officer to the President, arrived and immediately began to tell us how we should film. A few moments later, another crew arrived. 'They are going to film you filming the President,' we were told. 'For our own record'. Then, various other aides to the President arrived, one by one. Soon the garden room was so crowded that we could hardly move. Everyone insisted that their presence was essential.

Finally, General Musharraf made a dramatic entrance. He looked relaxed and greeted us warmly. While shaking his hand, I felt a strange tingle: the West had placed the burden of eradicating terrorism in these hands. I detected both confidence and determination in his eyes. The trouble was, I just did not trust him. The extremists were being fought, he told me, with 'enlightened moderation'. 'It's a two-pronged strategy.' Pakistan had to reject extremism and terrorism and opt for religious moderation and socio-economic development. The West, particularly, America had to change its foreign policy. The President went on and on about 'enlightened moderation'. He was somewhat taken aback when I suggested that perhaps the army itself was the biggest hurdle to his policy of '"enlightened moderation". The really closed minded Mullahs operate behind the scenes and wear the uniform of the military. He got very agitated when I suggested that perhaps Pakistan would be better off without him and went into a tirade against democracy.

When the interview finished, the President left without saying goodbye. General Sultan, who had been sitting behind him taking copious notes throughout the interview, called us over. He started to go through the interview line by line. 'Can you cut this sentence out,' he said. 'And that sentence, and this word in the sentence after that.' We looked at each other in utter amazement. We agreed to do whatever the General asked. Indeed, we threw 99 percent of the interview onto the cutting room floor and only kept his outburst against democracy.

As we were leaving Army House, General Sultan presented us a gift 'from the President'. It was a small, round, gold plated, weighty clock. Needless to say, given the choice, I would have opted for a good cricket bat.

V

Cricket plays an important part in the Pakistan of my memories. I have vivid memories of playing cricket and *guli danda*—a sort of ad hoc baseball where the improvised danda/bat takes determined aim at the equally eclectic guli/projectile—in the street with my cousins. It is essentially the Pakistan of my extended family. Without it, I would be a truncated human being. But this Pakistan is not based on some romanticised, non-existent past; the type we frequently encounter in fiction, such as Abe Kobo's gruelling *Besats Head for Home*, where the autobiographical narrator revisits scenes that exists only in his or her imagination. Kobo's protagonist, Kyuzo, is haunted by an absent past, a Japan he imagines but has never experienced. I, on the other hand, am energised by my childhood memories of Pakistan because they were experienced and real; they are as objective as the Indus School of Architecture in Karachi or the Kipling Museum in Lahore. Of course, the act of remembering—how we remember, what we remember, and indeed why we remember—is a complex process of negotiation with oneself. Selection, bias and poetic licence are involved. But what I recall of my own and hence Pakistan's past—reading the thrillers of 'Ibn Safi BA' to my grandfather, or trying to fathom the behaviour and mysteries of 'My Disappearing Uncle' Waheed—is exactly what attracts me to Pakistan. It is an intimate Pakistan, a humanised one. It is a past that makes the present bearable, and provides hope for the future.

Every visit 'back home', as the elders once used to say, has left vivid memories. I paid particular attention to what changed and what did not change. When I returned to Karachi after almost two decades, it was almost as I remembered it as a young boy. People everywhere, overcrowded buses, motor rickshaws weaving their way through alleys barely two metres wide. The roads were a bit wider than I remembered and there were many more concrete buildings. There were more cars on the road and the city's affluent district, Defence Colony, looked more out of place with the city as whole. But I could still find those huge camel carts carrying sacks of goods from the port to the city centre, from Kimari to Bunder Road, that I used to watch with delighted attention. As a child, I would run behind them and sometimes climb over them. The 'local' train still went around the city; it now appeared much slower, older and more polluting. On every visit, I saw a fatal accident involving the 'local', making me feel in familiar childhood territory. And another one involving two buses racing each other. The potholes around Memon Masjid were still there, except now they looked bigger and even more ancient—everyone knew the location of every single hole. Saddar, the prime focus of the city, hadn't changed a bit. The same bazaars, the same stalls, and narrow footpaths where individual entrepreneurs displayed their wares, leaving little space for the pedestrians. Even the cinemas remained as they were. Huge placards with gaudy paintings announced the current attractions. There always seemed to be more people outside the cinema than inside. But what really told me I was in Karachi was the unmistakable aroma—a heady mixture of exotic spices and exhaust fumes, human sweat and sweetmeats, dust and debris.

A PERSON OF PAKISTANI ORIGINS

Even around my Uncle Farid's house, where I usually stayed, the scent was piquant. An open sewer went around the house and then moved on to the adjacent homes. The smell from the drain combined with that from the papaya tree by the veranda to produce a distinctive aroma. I would find the whole family gathered to greet me. And the greetings and the hugs took quite some time. Then I would go to sit with Farid Mammu on his *charpoy*. 'Leave me alone with my nephew', he would say. 'He is back after all these years!' There was something in the way he uttered his words that actually said: 'You have never left. You were always here. Here right beside me.' Then he would turn to the pet parrot and try to teach him my name: 'Zia ... Zeeyaa'. 'He has better characteristics and is more reliable than most denizens of Karachi,' he would often say.

Like most of my family, Farid Mammu, my mother's elder brother, came to Pakistan in 1947 after Partition, leaving the little wealth his family had in India. He arrived in Karachi penniless but was fortunate enough to get a civil service appointment. Like his other brothers and sisters, he married within the family and had eight children in blocks of two. His two eldest sons only have two years between them; next come two girls also with two years between them. The girls are followed by a boy and a girl, also with two years between them. Finally, some ten years later, he had two more boys within two years. If one did not know better, one would confuse his children as four sets of twins. Apart from raising his own kids, Farid Mammu looked after his younger brother (my Uncle Waheed), his mother (my Nanni, who lived next door), and sisters, one of whom was in his care for a long time.

A few minutes with Farid Mammu and the conversation will move swiftly to his back. 'Oh!', he would say putting his hands on his sides and leaning backwards, 'there is no end to this pain'. I knew what was coming next: 'Press my back'. I would take my shoes off and climb on his *charpoy*. He would be laying face downwards with his arms stretched out. I would massage his back. 'Do you remember as an infant you used to jump all over my back? You used to walk from the tip of my toes right up to my neck. I remember. Then, what are you waiting for? You may be a few years older but I can still take your weight. Start at my toes.'

I would gently step on his toes and legs and massage them with my feet. He would close his eyes and relax, and my gaze would turn towards the courting geckos on the ceiling. I would remember another pair of geckos in another house, just as small and crowded as this one. But there instead of the open sewer circling the house, there was a rubbish tip just outside the door. Farid Mammu had just come back from work and announced that he was ill with TB.

There was a knock on the door. Someone shouted 'Milkman'. 'Pay the man,' Farid Mammu instructed one of his sons. 'Make sure he hasn't put too much water in the milk.' He would explain: 'it is part of his faith—*iman*—to dilute the milk.' Soon there was another, much louder, knock at the door. It was a woman asking for alms, a child clinging to her arms. Farid Mammu instructed one of his daughters to give the lady something to eat. No one ever left Farid Mammu's house empty handed. He had a particular weakness for widows and women with children. 'I know how difficult it is to raise children in Karachi,' he would openly acknowledge. 'I just don't know how people manage to survive in this city.'

How did Farid Mammu himself survive? When he was at the top of his salary scale he was making a miserable 2,000 rupees (around £100 in those days) a month. When one considers his family, plus the fact there was a mother and a younger brother to support, and that long queue of people knocking at the door, asking and getting help as a matter of faith, 2,000 rupees amounts to very little. Apart from food and rent, there were all those medical bills. Uncle Farid had taken everything the city could throw at him. Even going to and from work was a dangerous exercise. And he hated travelling in the city. 'Conveyance in Karachi,' he would say, 'is a big problem. To get on or off a bus, if you could find one, requires great dexterity and stamina. I don't have that type of energy any more.'

Every time I visited Karachi, I discovered the city had presented him with a new legacy. Now it was liver damage. Now kidney failure. Now a heart attack. And now cancer. He took everything with a smile, never really complained, either about his poor health or his misfortune and continued to work till it was physically impossible. Always wondering how those poor and less fortunate than him managed to survive. After years of hard work, he had little to show. His pension was less than half his final salary, and it was hardly adequate even to buy the basic necessities of survival. In any event it was not at all easy to collect. He had to go in person to collect it. And once, when he was too ill to walk and could not go himself, the pension office refused to pay. 'They are killing me before my time,' he announced and promptly undertook the long and dangerous journey to the pension office.

When I last saw Farid Mammu he had moved to a new house. 'The government has no rights on this house, my sons have built it,' he said proudly. And they did, brick by brick, step by step—it took almost three years to complete. He shared the house with two herds of buffaloes. The buffaloes, well over a score of them, flanked both the front and back of the house. The geckos still graced the ceiling, but the house was much bigger and almost every member of the family could find a corner to sleep.

Farid Mammu's Pakistan is an essential part of my mental landscape. I think, imagine and dream with it. Even the simplest of pleasures in this cerebral topography leave long, lingering recollections.

A PERSON OF PAKISTANI ORIGINS

I remember going with my one of cousins to the mosque for Friday prayers in Model Colony. After the prayers, we came out of the mosque and spent a considerable time looking for his shoes. 'I left them right here,' my cousins kept saying. 'No doubt you did,' I kept replying, while looking for my own shoes. I was spotted by a young man standing outside the mosque, supporting a wooden tray tied with a piece of string around his neck and holding a bunch of books under his left arm. He made a bee-line for me. 'You are from England,' he said. And without waiting for a reply: 'Would you like a paan, sir? I make the best paan around here.' I love paan: the betel leaf and areca nut concoction, with a host of other ingredients. But at that time I was more concerned with securing my shoes than eating a paan.

'No doubt you do,' I replied, without paying much attention to the young man.

'You know what Ibn Sina says about paan?' he tried to engage me in conversation. 'The paan has many properties. It is sour, bitter, hot, sweet, salty and astringent. It expels flatulence, removes bad odour, and beautifies the mouth, cleansing it while exciting voluptuous sensations. When the paan leaves are applied to the temples they relieve headache and pain, they can also be applied to painful and swollen glands to promote absorption, and to mammary glands to check the secretion of milk. Some scholars even claim that it is an aphrodisiac.'

'No doubt they do,' I nodded in apparent agreement.

'Did you know, sir, that paan is the most popular chewing gum in the Muslim World?' The man was undeterred. 'It is eaten all over the Indian Subcontinent. Even the Arabs love it. They call it *tanbul*. I make at least twelve different varieties of paan. In addition to lime, catechu and finely chopped betelnuts I can also add cardamoms, nutmegs, cloves, camphor, aniseed and a number of other aromatics. I can make it sweet, sour or my speciality the *asmani* paan—it will take you straight to heaven'.

'No doubt it will.' By now I had forgotten about my shoes. I was really impressed by the erudite persistence of this young person who, I gathered, was a student, as he was carrying books with him.

'You are not convinced, sir. Perhaps you have been reading in the papers that paan causes cancer and such diseases. The paan leaf contains volatile acid, lime is an irritant, and catechu and betelnut have alkaloids. This is true to some extent. But you should know that all the acids and alkalis in paan can be neutralised with the addition of good things such as coconut and almonds. I make a very scientific paan, sir. Which one would you like?'

I couldn't help smiling. 'All right, then. I will take your special *asmani* paan.'

The young man made the paan, rolled it neatly and offered it to me. 'Don't chew it at once. Just let the juice circulate naturally in your mouth,' he offered as parting advice. Without looking at its contents, I popped it in my mouth and gave him a rupee.

We eventually found our shoes and decided to return home in a rickshaw. There were several standing outside the mosque. We jumped into one. The congregation was spilling out of the mosque and the road was totally congested. The rickshaw was not moving, but I was. Suddenly my head started to spin. The entire traffic began to revolve around me. I had eaten paan many times before, but never anything like this. I wanted to spit it out, but the sensation was as pleasurable as it was nasty. Strange images began to float in front of my eyes as though I was watching a motion picture. I could see myself as a child having the stalk of the betel leaf, smeared in oil, administered to my rectum to induce my bowels to behave themselves. I could see my grandmother chewing a special paan and then spitting the remains, with the help of a cheese cloth, in my aching ear. My cousin noticed things were not quite as they should be. He asked the rickshaw driver to manoeuvre himself towards what looked like a recently white washed wall. I could see it was the only unspoilt wall for miles around. The rickshaw driver managed to get quite close to the fortification.

'Go on,' said my cousin. 'Perform the ritual.'

I freely ejected the spittle onto the shining surface. The projection landed in a splat and then formed an arc as though it was a blood stain left by a wounded man using the wall for support as he falls down unconscious.

'He put tobacco in your paan. Patti number 33. It's the strongest tobacco there is,' my cousin informed me, as the rickshaw driver maundered to re-join the traffic.

'No doubt he did'. I could barely get the words out of my mouth.

Even today, if I close my eyes, I can taste that *asmani* paan. Just as I can remember, quite vividly, a late summer afternoon I spent with my Uncle Muqeet, the younger brother of my mother-in-law, in Lahore. The sun was in a vengeful mood and we were amongst its main victims. Both of us were completely drenched in sweat. Anywhere but in Lahore, this kind of scorching heat would keep people firmly indoors.

Every day, after returning from his school, where he was deputy headmaster, Uncle Muqeet would go out to give private tuition to some of his students. That day, he was going to teach one of his pupils in Township, which is a few kilometres from Model Town where he lived. I was accompanying him because he had promised to take me back to Gulburg, an affluent part of the city where I was staying with another one of my uncles, after finishing his tuition. In Lahore only the main streets seem to have names. While I could have returned to Gulburg on my own, I would never have found the exact *khoti* where I was staying. I had visions of wandering about in Gulberg for hours looking for the right building. So when Uncle Muqeet suggested he could take me back, I immediately accepted his offer.

A PERSON OF PAKISTANI ORIGINS

Normally, Uncle Muqeet moved around on his scooter. But it had been stolen a few days ago and we had to take a bus. We had waited for a considerable time, under the burning sun, for our ride to arrive. But eventually the bus turned up and dropped us right in front of the house of Uncle Muqeet's pupil. It was a poorly built dwelling. It seemed to have a curious external structure: four whitewashed walls, curved rather than straight, and a roof which was bigger than the parameters of the walls. Uncle Muqeet knocked on the door. I looked around the street. There were several *thalay wallahs* selling fruits and vegetables. Bicycles and scooters were parked everywhere. A group of children were playing cricket, with a real cricket ball, in the middle of the street. Passers-by had to duck the ball as the bowlers delivered it at great speed to the batsman and as it flew, equally ferociously, off the bat. If they succeeded in missing the ball, they had to push and shove their way between the stalls and dodge the bicycles and rickshaws moving in all directions. I marvelled at the fact no one seemed to be bothered about anything—despite the enormously high chance of being hit by the flying cricket ball, knocked over by a bicycle, crushed by a rickshaw, turning over a vegetable or fruit stall, everyone moved unconcerned, successfully dodging everything and everyone. The chaos was controlled. The apparent anarchy was well orchestrated.

Uncle Muqeet knocked at the door again.

'They must be resting,' he said.

He knocked at the door once again. Still there was no reply. This time he knocked at the door with some enthusiasm. The door came off its hinges and would surely have landed on our head with menaces had it not been held by its handle by someone from the inside. A man in his vest and pyjama picked up the door and put it aside. Then he turned to Uncle Muqeet.

'Master Shahib,' he said politely, 'I have told you many times not to knock on the door so hardly. You should know this is a government house.'

Uncle Muqeet smiled, said nothing, and went inside.

If it was hot outside, it was an inferno inside. Both of us continued to sweat even more profusely. A teenage boy arrived with some books and sat in one corner of the room. Uncle Muqeet joined him and immediately started a biology lesson.

The man in the vest and pyjama asked me to sit down. I sat on a small, wobbly, wooden chair. He brought Uncle Muqeet and I a glass of water, and then came and sat next to me. The water was rather warm. It only increased my thirst and perspiration.

'Please forgive me, we don't have an electric fan,' the man said. 'But would you like a hand fan?'

I nodded as if to say 'yes'.

The man started to look around the floor. Eventually he found something, picked it up and handed it to me. It was an old, tattered hand fan consisting of a small stick stuck in a rectangular piece of jute matting. I started to wave the fan randomly and widely to generate some air. But it did little to ease my discomfort.

'You know we have learned from experience that it is not very productive to shake the fan about like that,' the man said, gently slapping me on my shoulder. He took the fan from my hand. 'It is more productive to hold the fan in front of you, and shake your face vigorously.' He proceeded to demonstrate: 'like this'.

I looked at him in disbelief. He slapped me on the shoulder again.

'Joke, only a joke! But you got to have a sense of humour to survive in this country. Master Shahib has a great sense of humour. Someone stole his scooter and he prayed that the thief would have enough sense to check the brakes!'

Uncle Muqeet paid no attention to the man and continued with his lesson. 'Yes, my dear sir, a sense of humour. All we can do is to laugh at our poverty and the greed and incompetence of our politicians. We can hope that things will improve, but the system here is not designed for improvement. It is not geared to help poor folk like me. Only education provides us with an outside chance to get out of this trap. Education is our only weapon. That's why I want my son to go to College. God bless Master Shahib he comes all the way from Model Town to give extra lessons to my son.'

Uncle Muqeet seemed completely unaware of what was being said or happening around him. He was too preoccupied with the lesson. The man continued. 'Without that hope, that slender hope that my son will go to College, obtain good qualifications, get a job and get his parents out of this misery, I cannot exist. It is the only hope that pushes me on. This is why I spend all my meagre income on his education. Please forgive me that there is no electric fan in my house. That I cannot offer you good chairs to sit on. But, you see, the choice I have is either to buy these things or have my son educated.' I was quite moved by the man's oration. Suddenly, the hot sweaty room became a pleasant enclave. The wobbly wooden chair turned into a comfortable sofa.

VI

There is little comfort in the lives of the vast majority of the poor in Pakistan. For the religiously minded, Islam is the only balm against the harsh realities of grinding poverty and deprivation. The malfunctioning State itself provides little help. Even getting a 'Nadra card', that confirms their Pakistani identity, can be a galling experience.

In the summer of 2011, I came across Nadeem Ahmad, an affable boy in his late-teens. He lived in the remote 'village number 44' in the Shah Koat district of Punjab, near Lahore, and attended the village's Kotla Khawan School, where the teachers describe him as a model pupil. Despite being orphaned at an early age, and with numerous responsibilities for his siblings, he

47

worked hard and obtained over 70 percent in his Class 8 assessment. Encouraged by his results, he threw himself into the preparation for his Class 9 examination.

But just a few weeks before the examination, Nadeem was told he could not be allowed to take his examination. He did not have the appropriate identity papers and was not registered with the National Database and Registration Authority (Nadra) as a Pakistani citizen. More specifically, he needed a 'Form B' which was mandatory for sitting Class 9 examination. In other words, he was not a person of Pakistani origins.

Nadeem went to the local offices of Nadra. But the officials refused to entertain his request for Form B. There was a specific problem. Form B can only be obtained by parents on behalf of their children. Without parents, he was told, there was no way of obtaining the form. Indeed, he was a person with no identity. 'I visited the Nadra office so many times that I became disoriented,' he said. 'But they simply refused to make my Form B.'

Angry and frustrated, Nadeem wrote a letter, on 30 November 2010, to the Children's Complaint Office of the Ombudsman in Islamabad. 'I ask you,' he wrote, 'is it my fault that my parents are dead? Why am I being punished for an act of God? Now I am beginning to think that our beloved country prefers that I become a labourer. Is there no one in this country who can throw a rope of hope towards the orphans? How ironic that our own laws are destroying the future of our own children! Is there no limit to the cruelty that can be perpetrated on the children of this country?' Nadeem's letter landed on the desk of Saleem Durrani, my cousin, who was then Child Complaint Advisor at the Ombudsman Regional Office in Lahore. 'I was moved to tears when I read the letter,' my cousin told me. 'It was beautifully written, full of pertinent questions, by someone clearly accomplished and very talented.'

The Ombudsman of Pakistan has a specific mandate to investigate complaints against any Federal Agency. Its independent complaints handling service is free and open to everyone. In the Lahore Office, located on the third floor of an office building on Davis Road, anyone including children can walk in to complain against government agencies. It is one of the busiest Ombudsman offices in the country, handling over 13,000 complaints in 2009. But it has no real budget. Indeed, even the position of the Ombudsman in Lahore has been vacant for months. The office is actually run by eight advisors, mostly retired civil servants, who cover different areas, such as women's rights and the rights of children.

Even though Pakistan ratified the UN Convention of the Rights of the Child in 1990, children are amongst the most neglected segment of society. 40 percent of children of school going age remain out of school, more than half are girls. 50 percent who do go to school dropout—largely because of widespread physical abuse. Some 30 million children are forced into child labour. Children as young as seven and eight have been used and trained by Pakistani Taliban to become suicide bombers. Sexual exploitation of children is rampant. There are a number of laws to protect child rights, such as the Punjab Children Act 1983, but no one pays any attention to these laws. The future of Pakistan is thus being systemically destroyed.

Durrani, a stocky man who smiles generously, wrote to the Secretary of the Board of Intermediate and Secondary Education on behalf of Nadeem. He received a bureaucratic reply stating that a Form B was essential for acquiring the 'unique registration number' for the examination, which itself was necessary 'so that the candidate may not be able to deceive the examination system by getting double registration in two different (exam) boards'. As Nadeem had not followed the law, his 'complaint is liable to be dismissed'. Letters to Nadra produced similar results.

But Durrani persisted. 'I was prepared to take the case to the governor if necessary,' he said. He also started exploring other avenues to confirm Nadeem's identity. Eventually he discovered that his father, Bashir Ahmad, had an account at a local branch of Habib Bank in Shah Koat district. The bank manager agreed to write a letter to Nadra confirming that Nadeem was the son of the late Bashir Ahmad. But Nadra wanted this 'Original Guardianship Certificate' to be verified by a court. This was eventually done. So finally, in May 2011, after six months of dogged persistence by Durrani, Nadeem obtained his coveted 'Form B'. He sat his Class 9 exam in August 2011 and passed with excellent results.

I was bowled over by Nadeem. Here was an orphaned teenager, looking after his siblings all on his own, with an admirable passion for education. When you travel throughout Pakistan you meet lots of people like this—folks who manage somehow to remain unsoiled, keep their garb clean, while striding purposefully through a briny of smut and corruption. It is their Pakistan that I love and identify with.

It was this affection that motivated me to make another effort to secure a Pakistani Origin Card. I was also encouraged by the reply from High Commissioner, Syed Ibne Abbas, to my 'distressing scenes and the High Commission' email. 'Thank you very much for sharing your concerns with me about our consular services,' he wrote. 'Your unpleasant experience yesterday at the High Commission saddens me. I will most definitely be looking into all the points you have raised to improve the situation and services. I am determined to fix issues you have rightly pointed out. You would agree with me that I cannot change a life time of attitudes in a quick fix. It will take time! Nevertheless, I assure you that this sort of conduct from any member of my staff will not be tolerated and is unacceptable. I assure you that I will be looking in to this in all earnest.'

So on a rainy day in May 2017, accompanied by my wife, and with all the necessary documents in hand, I went again to the

A PERSON OF PAKISTANI ORIGINS

High Commission. I was pleasantly encouraged to note that the process had improved considerably. The 'scrutiny' counter had been replaced with a comfortable seating room for waiting applicants. After an initial check, aspirants were ushered into a large room with desks neatly arranged and numbered. You start with the first desk where your documents are examined. Then the next desk where your details are input in a digital system and your photograph is taken. Then the desk after that where you are asked to check a printout of your digital application to make sure all is correct. And finally the last desk where you provide your application and service fee and are given a receipt. The process went like clockwork for my wife. At the end of the process she was given a tracking number and told that she would receive her Card in about six weeks. In fact, her Nadra 'Smart Card' arrived within a month. There was a short letter attached. 'Dear Customer,' it read, 'please help us improve our service. If you experienced any discourtesy or misbehaviour at our centre, please inform us by visiting...'

My application did not fare so well. The Pakistani passports of my father and mother, and their respective ID cards, as well all affidavits and other paraphernalia from my relatives in Pakistan, were not good enough to prove my identity as a person of Pakistani origins. I needed a birth certificate. I thought that I should explain that when I was born in Dipalpur, in a small village on the Pakistani side of the Indian-Pakistani border, things were not all that clear cut. The two countries were engaged in another round of their everlasting enmities and my parents decided to let things settle before registering my precocious arrival. As they were trying to adjust to their new place of residence, they got busy, and a few years passed by before they remembered the need to register my, by now prodigious, existence. When they did recall, my mother despatched my father to the local district council office to register my birth. What happed next is described in my book, *Balti Britain*:

51

The registration office was in Okara, a tiring train journey from where we lived. It took my father over a day to find the relevant place by which time he had forgotten the actual date of birth. He knew it had a three in it, but could not remember whether it was the 3rd, 13th, 23rd, 30th or 31st of October. He settled on the last number in the sequence for his firstborn son. But worse followed: he was vague on whether this momentous event, to which I rushed to with such despatch, occurred in 1951 or 1952. Here he opted for 1951 thinking, as he later told me, 'it is better for you to be older than younger'. On his return journey, however, my father was caught in one of those seasonal rainstorms which turn everything into a large paddy field. He arrived home drenched, heavily decorated with mud, but proudly clutching my birth certificate. When my mother examined it she was aghast. She gave a loud, high pitched, shrill scream— the sort she still utters when confronted by incomprehensible horror. The birth certificate, written in Indian ink, had been washed clean by the perfidious rain. At first sight, it was void of detail. But it had been written with a hard, wooden pen which, if the certificate were manipulated carefully in a good light, had left indentations on the thick paper. After painstaking scrutiny, my mother could, just about, make out my name and a 3 where the date was supposed to be.

The atmosphere at the High Commission was genial but not amenable to complex explanations and tangled stories. So I just shrugged my shoulders and said 'Sorry, I do not have a birth certificate.'

I was sent to another room where I had to fill in an 'Application Form for National Status Verification'. My details were taken again, my documents photocopied, attested and neatly stuffed into a file. 'It will all be sent to Pakistan for authentication,' the polite officer said.

I was given a reference number. 'If it all goes well,' I was told, 'you should hear something in a year or so.'

I am still waiting. I suspect my Pakistani origins are destined to remain ambiguous.

2.

••••••••

IBN SAFI, BA

••••••••

1

When I visited Bahwalnagar in May 1975, I found little had changed. A new generation of *goll guppa-wallas, chaat-wallas* and *paan-wallas* had taken over the stalls in Railway Bazaar. It was still the direct route from the Railway Station to our house in the centre of the town, where we lived and I grew up. I had left the city at the age of nine, when my parents migrated to London. And I expected no one would know me. Indeed, they did not know me. But they recognised me: I was the returning grandson of Hakim Sahib.

Abdur Razziq Khan, known locally and affectionately simply as 'Hakim Sahib', was one of the most distinguished citizens of the town. I called him Nana. He hated the Raj and the British with equal measure. Not least because the British had outlawed his profession: *hikmat*, or traditional Islamic medicine. He looked after his mostly rural patients from his surgery, 'Haziq Dawa Khana', which was situated in the middle of Railway Bazaar. Everyone in Bahwalnagar knew him, and everyone knew that his grandson had come from England to visit him.

I had arrived the previous night and it was my first day in Bahwalnagar. Nana had asked me to meet him at his surgery after lunch. 'And bring a copy of the latest ibn-e-Safi with you,' he had instructed.

I knew ibn Safi well. During my childhood in Bahwalnagar, the entire extended family, consisting of scores of uncles and aunties, were addicted to ibn-e-Safi. We read ibn Safi and had ibn Safi read to us. He published two best-selling series of Urdu spy novels. The first, *Jasoosi Dunya* (Spy World), featured two detectives: Colonel Ahmad Kamal Faridi, the exceptionally clever and highly ethical Chief of Police, and his partner and assistant Sajid Hameed, a humorous and playful young man who appears to be careless, but in fact has great presence of mind. The second, the 'Imran series,' featured Ali Imran: a playful, highly intelligent detective who is also a master of disguise. Two novels came out every month; there was always a new ibn Safi to read every fortnight. Nana had assigned a cupboard in the house where all our ibn Safis were stored, and I was proudly put in charge of this treasure. It was also my responsibility to secure the new novels as soon as they hit the street. I remember that at a tender age of seven or eight, I had to fight my way through the crowds that always gathered in front of newspaper vendors and street sellers to buy the latest adventures of 'Hameedi-Faridi' and Imran.

I set off for Nana's surgery at about three o'clock. As I walked on Railway Bazaar, I was beckoned by the *paan-walla*. 'Young Sahib, young Sahib,' he shouted, 'you are the grandson of Hakim Sahib. Right? I will make a special *paan* for you—in your honour.'

It is practically impossible to escape a *paan-walla* anywhere in Pakistan. *Paan* is the heart-shaped leaf of the betel plant, a type of creeper, on to which a number of spices are smothered, seeds and nut are added, and the complete concoction is then folded into a triangular shape. It has three basic ingredients: *katha*, a reddish solution of the heart-wood of the tree Acacia Catechu Wild; *choona*, lime paste; and *chalia*, areca nut (which in botanical terms is not a nut, but a seed), which is also known as *supari*. Beyond these, a whole range of different spices, seeds, nuts and dried fruit can be added to give the *paan* specific taste and flavour. The most visible ingredient of *paan* is the *katha* which produces natural red colour. Folklore has it that paan was popularised by Queen Noorjehan, the mother of Mughal Emperor

Shahjehan who built the Taj Mahal as a symbol of his love for his wife, Mumtaz Mahal. Noorjehan used *paan*, presumably with a lot of *katha* in it, as a lipstick! In Bahwalnagar, lipstick coloured spit graces most of the city's walls, particularly if they have been recently white washed.

The *paan-walla* picked a betel leaf from a tray, carefully dried it, covered it with *katha* with a round spoon, dropped a little *choona* on one side, and placed a small pinch of *chalia* in the middle. 'Not too much *chalia*,' I said. 'And make it small pieces. I find them too difficult to chew; I don't want to break my teeth.' 'Do not worry Sahib,' the *paan-walla* replied, as he continued to add other ingredients: cardamom, aniseed, grated coconut, cloves, rose essence, chutney... Eventually he handed me the *paan*.

'My best! I call it Divine *paan*. Direct from the heavens through me to you.' I took the *paan* and placed it in my mouth: it simply melted away.

II

Ibn-e-Safi BA is as indigenous to Pakistan, and as ubiquitous, as *paan*. His real name was Asrar Ahmad; the 'BA' in his *nom de plume* was integral. When Asrar Ahmad obtained his Bachelor of Arts from Agra University, in the late 1940s, it was still rare for a Muslim to be so highly educated. He was born in the small village of Nara in Allahabad, India, on 26 July 1928. He published his first detective story in 1948 in a magazine called *Nikhat*, which was printed in Allahabad. He then went on to write under various pseudonyms, eventually settling for ibn-e-Safi BA after the success of his *Shola* (spark) series. He was a progressive writer, deemed subversive, and branded as such both by the British and then the Indian authorities after them. Warrants were issued for his arrest and he ended up escaping to Pakistan. *Jasoosi Dunya* began in India in 1952; the Imran series was launched in Pakistan in 1958. Ibn Safi published his novels simultaneously in India and Pakistan, and kept the Subcontinent enthralled till his death by cancer, age 52, on 26 July 1980 (coincidently the same date as his birthday). He left some 232 novels behind him. A whole generation of Pakistanis grew up on his writing, idolising Hameed, Farid and Imran. This vast output took its toll and in the middle of his career, between 1961 and 1963, ibn-e-Safi developed schizophrenia. But he recovered to make a sensational comeback, with the bestselling Imran novel, *Dairrh Matwaalay*.

Like *paan*, ibn Safi novels have three basic ingredients. First, there is the language—the *katha*. Ibn-e-Safi writes with wit and panache, taking great pleasure at word play. Imran frequently quotes and misquotes the great Urdu poets Ghalib and Mir, as well as Confucius, to poke fun at himself. The dialogue is always crisp, scintillating, and punctuated with layer upon layer of innuendos and puns. Yet, nothing is overwritten; everything is precise and measured. Even the titles of the novels play with words: *Larazti Lakeeran* (Shivering Lines), *Adhura Admi* (Unfinished Man), *Tabut Main Chikh* (Scream of Iron) and *Lash Gati Raay?* (The Singing Corpse). And the villains are just delicious: Qalandar Bayabani, the spy story teller; Theresia Bumble-Bee of Bohemia, who behaves like a chameleon; Gerald Shashtri, the western expert in Sanskrit; and the most ingenious and treacherous of all, Sing Hee. Second, the emphasis on virtue—the *choona*. Ibn-e-Safi was a highly moral man who took religious virtue seriously. Although religion itself is never mentioned in the novels, his protagonists are highly ethical, indeed critical Muslims: they follow the law impeccably, do not believe in unnecessary violence, do not drink or gamble, and they never, never have sex. Even when the playful Hameed and naughty Imran are surrounded by irresistible glamour—in five star hotels, for example—they are not allowed even a side-ways glance at desirable pulchritude however enticingly displayed. Moreover, they are thoroughly professional, exceptionally rational and precise in their actions. The virtues are not overplayed, or thickly layered; they are just there, a natural and integral part of his characters. They should be, ibn-e-Safi seems to suggest, the norms of Muslim society. Third, the plot—the *supari*. While the plots are crafted deftly, the pleasure in reading ibn-e-Safi is not so much in discovering the mystery that will eventually resolve itself at the end, but how the drama is unfolded, how the story is weaved, and how the familiar set-pieces are manipulated and twisted not just to surprise but to delight. Ibn-e-Safi wants his readers to be involved with his creation, to appreciate how the narrative is put together, to enjoy how his familiar tropes perform in unfamiliar situations, savour the texture and every morsel of the story.

Then there is the *paan* leaf itself: the landscape of the story. The novels are set in an unnamed country. We know, however, that Hameedi-Fradi are defending India. But it is an India that stretches from the North West Frontier to the Far East, and it is seen as a civilisation rather than a nation state. The Imran series is clearly set in Pakistan—but it is not a Pakistan that we would recognise. Ibn-e-Safi's Pakistan is a confident nation with unimpeachable integrity. And his characters are at ease everywhere. The entire globe is 'home'. The protagonists travel all over the world in pursuit of the villains (who invariably tend to be white men): plague-infected ghettos in the US; colonial settlements in South Africa; the congested streets of cities in England; and, a fictional country known as Zero Land (where, naturally, everyone is a non-entity). There is also an awareness of progress and of the future. In the 1957 novel *Toofan Ka Aghwa* (Hurrican Kidnap), we find a loveable robot, 'Fauladmi', who performs household chores, controls traffic, and even settles minor disputes between citizens. But Ibn-e-safi is also aware of the downside of technology. In *Jungle Ki Aag* (Jungle Fire), written in the

1960, the villain invents a machine that turns three crippled beggars into a gorilla.

Before I could thank the *paan-walla*, I was assaulted by two young boys. One pulled my arms; the other was firmly attached to my right leg. They were intent on moving me in two different directions. It took some effort to disentangle myself and control the enthusiasm of the boys. 'Sahib! Sahib!' the boy attached to my arm was urging me to the *goll guppa* stall. And for old time's sake, why not?

'Only one *goll guppa*, please!' I pleaded with the *goll guppa-walla*. '*Teek hai, Teek hai* (ok), just for today. One is enough to get you hooked.' I opened my mouth as widely as possible, prepared to receive his bounty. But he recoiled in horror. 'No sir!', he said. 'Never! Never will I be putting my divine *goll guppa* in a mouth full of *paan*.' I quickly spat the remaining *paan* from my mouth; drank a few sips of tamarind water from the small glass he placed in my hands. 'Now you are ready for the *goll guppa* experience,' he said exultantly, and carefully placed a large *goll guppa*, full of chickpeas and tamarind water, in my mouth. As the *goll guppa* exuded its divinity in my mout, I found my body encrusted with a new effusion of boys all anxious to drag bits of my being in sundry directions. I manage to wriggle out and ran towards a bookseller. His wares were displayed on the street next to a pharmacy. He sat on a stool, a fan in his hand, surrounded by books and magazine. There were several Ibn-e-Safi novels neatly displayed.

As far as I know, *goll guppa* is a totally *desi*, that is local, concoction. Not unlike Ibn-e-Safi novels. Arrogant and ill-informed Pakistani literati have dismissed his work as derivative, not worthy of serious attention. He is said to have borrowed from Arthur Conan Doyle, Leslie Charteris, Ian Fleming and a host of others. Such dismissal says a great deal about the deep inferiority complex one detects in the Pakistani literati. Imagination is not something that Pakistanis, the *desis*, are allowed to have. The *desi* is always seen as inferior to the 'western'. Of course, there are shades of Bond in Ibn-e-Safi just as there are shades of Bond in Robert Ludlum's Bourne novels. It's a genre, for God's sake. In any case, by the time Ian Fleming published the first James Bond novel, *Casino Royale* (under the title *You Asked For It*) in 1953, Ibn-e-Safi had already published well over a dozen novels in the *Jasoosi Dunya* series and the characters and adventures of 'Hamidi-Faridi' had been well established. While Bond certainly knows his drinks, his gadgets and his weapons, Ibne Safi's characters are more at home with Freudian psychology, Nietzsche, Confucius and Omar Khayyam. 'The Saint' may be as suave as Imran, but his adventures are mundane and he cannot match Imran's ability to disguise himself or dodge bullets.

Ibn-e-Safi's literary output is about as Pakistani or Indian as one can get. No doubt, like most of us, he was influenced by what he read. He was honest enough to acknowledge those who influenced him. But *Jasoosi Dunya* and *Imran series* are part of a very specific genre of Urdu literature that played with magical realism centuries before magical realism was invented. The genre can be traced back to the sixteenth century and to such classical novels as *Dastan-e Ameer Hamza* ('The Narrative of Ameer Hamza') and *Talism-e Hoshruba* ('The Magic That Robs the Wits'; translated by Shahnaz Aijazuddin as *The Enchantment of the Senses*). These are sprawling narratives of kings and Jinns, battles and romances, moral imperatives and ethical choices, deeply rooted in the imagination and the soil of the Subcontinent—just like the *goll guppas*. Ibn-e-Safi's plots are as multi-layered, complex, and convoluted as the stories in *Talism-e Hoshruba*.

III

'Do you have the latest ibn-e-Safi?' I asked the bookseller.

'Yes, Sahib,' he shot back. 'The latest and the original.'

'Original?' I was intrigued.

'Yes, Sahib. You can't be too careful nowadays. There are vandals out there who produce fake copies of his work. Ibn-e-Safi has himself complained. But they don't listen.'

'Here,' he said, handing me a novel, '*Khooni Panja* (Blood Claw). Hot off the press.'

I bought the novel and ran all the way to Haziq Dawakhana.

Hakim Sahib was sitting cross-legged on a cushion listening attentively to a patient. I composed myself. I took a seat near him, keeping a respectable distance from the private space between a hakim and his *mareez*, the patient. When he finished, Nana looked up.

'I see you have got the latest ibn-e-Safi.'

He paused for a thought. 'Can you still read Urdu?'

'I think I can,' I replied.

'Then begin at the beginning.'

Khooni Punja was from the Imran series. The comical and apparently incompetent Ali Imran, 27, Oxford PhD, also known as X-2, lives in a modest flat with his three faithful employees: his cook, the cook's wife, and his personal body guard, Joseph, an African. Handsome and a flamboyant dresser, he speaks several languages, and is an expert in a number of fighting arts. When he has to fight, he fights like Jackie Chan: aiming to humiliate the opponent into submission rather than physically beating them up. He is a master of the Chinese 'Sung Art', which he learned from one of his arch enemies, Sung Hee, a Chinese criminal and spy. Imran has a string of agents working for him, but they do not know his identity; whenever any of his subordinates are in trouble X-2 appears mysteriously, as if he were a 'spirit', to save them. The most fearsome of his criminal opponents, Theresa Bumble Bee of Bohemia (T3B), is deeply in love with him. At the beginning of each novel, Imran appears in disguise as some insignificant character in the background, ever present, but almost invisible. The readers themselves do not know it is Imran until well into the novel. What we do know is that an elaborate trap is being set. And we may suspect there is more to that beggar with the twisted body who insists on praising Allah incessantly, or the *paan-walla* who is trying to attract customers by juggling his 'Asmani *paan*', or the incompetent motor mechanic who is taking forever to change a wheel.

'Well, get on with it then!' Hakim Sahib jogged me from my reverie.

I had forgotten to read, and I was struggling a bit with my Urdu.

'It is possible that this event would not have happened. Or it would have. We cannot be sure that the riot was not used as a front for something else. It started innocently enough and then developed into wide scale looting. Shops were vandalised. Paan-wallas and goll guppa-wallas were robbed.'

'What?' Hakim Sahib asked sharply. 'Read that again.'

'Shops were vandalised. Paan-wallas and goll guppa-wallas were robbed.'

'Carry on.'

'Maybe we can say that another event was unfolding behind the riot. The initial impulse for the troubles was provided by the bulky man, with an ill-fitting suit, eating ravenously in the restaurant. A young couple arrived and sat in front of him. He looked at them while placing a handful of rice in his mouth. The girl was exceptionally beautiful. Did she look at him? Qasim did not know her. But he knew the man accompanying her. He was the son of a well-to-do businessman. He really liked the girl. Did she look towards him again? Qasim tried to ignore the couple and concentrate on his food. His eye was caught by a Pathan, sitting at one end of the restaurant. Wearing an ostentatious shalwar kameez, in bright blue shades, the Pathan had finished his meal. The waiter brought him some coffee and biscuits. The Pathan dunked a biscuit in the coffee and ate it as though he was performing an act of high ritual significance.'

'What? What?' Hakim Sahib leaned forward as if he hadn't quite heard what I read. 'Read that again.'

The waiter brought him some coffee and biscuits. The Pathan dunked a biscuit in the coffee and ate it as though he was performing an act of high ritual significance.

'Carry on.'

Qasim became aware that the couple were laughing at him. He tried to ignore them. But then they started pointing at him. They were openly mocking and humiliating him. Qasim just could not take it anymore. He picked up the chair next to him and threw it at the young man. Within minutes the restaurant was engulfed in an all-out brawl. Chairs, tables, plates, shoes—everything was flying. The brawl spilled out into the street. And the fight in the restaurant turned into a riot in the bazaar.

I paused a minute to make sure Hakim Sahib was still attentive. He was. But there was a slightly troubled look on his face. 'Why have you stopped?' he said. 'Carry on'.

Inside the restaurant, the lights went off. Everything fell into darkness. There was a scream. "Let me go, let me go", yelled a woman. It looked as though someone was trying to suffocate her. When the light came back a few minutes later, the young girl had disappeared. Her companion was lying on the floor, bleeding profusely. He had been stabbed. Qasim had been knocked unconscious. The restaurant was in total disarray. But the Pathan still sat on his table at the corner. He surveyed the scene. "Array baap ray", he said. "What a mess!"

'That's enough, that's enough,' Hakim Sahib shouted. He was agitated. 'I have heard enough. Where is my walking stick?'

I got up and handed the walking stick to him. 'Come with me,' he said. 'And bring that wretched novel with you.'

Hakim Sahib closed the door of his surgery. Walking stick in his left hand, he set off at a determined pace, with me walking as fast as I could to keep up. As we passed other shops in the bazaar people turned to watch the parade and quickly ascertained Hakim Sahib was not in a very good mood. 'Something agitating you Hakim Sahib?' asked one. Hakim Sahib gave no acknowledgement but carried on walking, brandishing his stick with a no nonsense swagger. Soon people started to follow us. After twenty minutes or so, we arrived at a large, dilapidated house. Hakim Sahib knocked at the huge wooden door with his walking stick. There was no reply. Hakim Sahib knocked again. 'Master Chaudhry, Master Chaudhry, come out,' he declaimed. 'There is no point hiding from me!'

A window, adjacent to the large door, opened. A man, in a *dhoti* but naked from the waist upwards, leaned forward. 'Oh Merciful God,' he said, 'is everything all right? Hakim Sahib you look too agitated. You should think of your heart at your age.'

'My heart is stronger than your brain,' Hakim Sahib shot back. 'If I have told you once, I have told you a thousand times. Have I not?'

'What Hakim Sahib, what?'

'Not to peddle your fake novels Master Chaudhry!'

Hakim Sahib grabbed the novel from my hand. 'This, this trash. *Khooni Punja*. This is one of yours, isn't it? Why do you have to disgrace the good name of Ibn-e-Safi BA.'

'But, but... Hakim Sahib'.

'No buts'.

'But, but...Hakim Sahib how did you know?'

The question transformed Hakim Sahib. He became calm. 'Oh, Master Chaudhry,' he said. 'It is so obvious. Ibne Safi would never cause a riot in a street for a kidnapping to be staged in a restaurant. That's just grotesque violence. You have tried—unsuccessfully—to combine the opening sequences of two Imran novels: *Lash ka Qahqa* ('Laughter of the Corpse') and *Mahaktay Muhafiz* ('Cheeky Protectors'). Anyway, who would want to rob the poor *goll guppa-walla?*

A PERSON OF PAKISTANI ORIGINS

'Those who want to eat the *goll guppas*!'

'Just shut up, Master Chaudhry and listen. This was not your cardinal mistake. Your unforgivable sin was to give Imran's identity away right at the beginning of the novel. Don't you know that only Imran says *"Array baap ray"* (Holy Father)—that is his *takya kalam* (pet phrase). The moment someone says *"Array baap ray"*, the reader knows it is Imran in disguise. And Imran never, never dunks his biscuit in his coffee. With or without high ritual significance. He is a tea drinker.'

'I am really sorry, Hakim Sahib.' Master Chaudhry slipped a *kurta* over his head and came out. 'I cannot apologise enough for causing you so much distress. Please accept my sincere apologies for the same. Next time I will try and do much better.'

'What do you mean next time? There will be no next time. Next time you will put your own name on your own trash.'

'But Hakim Sahib no one buys novels with my name on them. Ibn-e-Safi sells. I have to try and make a living somehow!'

Hakim Sahib became reflective. 'That's true,' he replied. 'People do not appreciate *desi* literature. Particularly when it is so bad.' He paused for thought. 'Ok then, if you are determined to have a career writing fake novels, make sure you don't give the game away on the first two pages. But try and keep your hands off our national writers. This *farangi* fellow, what's him name, Sheikh Spear, fake his books. Who knows? You may capture an international market!'

2012

3.

········

TWO BOOKS
AND AN AUNTIE

········

1

Most South Asian families have one. An Auntie Ji, who is not really a member of the family, but everyone's Auntie. On the Subcontinent they serve as marriage brokers and go-betweens, and keep the neighbourhood well-oiled with gossip. Amongst the Asian diaspora in Britain, the universal Auntie Ji performed an additional function: she served as a local moral guardian who kept a beady eye on the young. During the 1960s and 1970s, when the British Muslim community was finding its feet and mosques were few, the neighbourhood Auntie was a powerful figure. She would visit the households of her district judiciously, dispensing religious and social advice, occasionally giving Qur'anic lessons to children, and serving, when necessary, as a marriage guidance councillor. The Auntie Ji of Clapton Pond in East London, where I grew up, was called Auntie Rashida. A tall, dark woman, she was, in the company of other women, an exceptionally graceful and tender person. But when it came to men, she was transformed, approaching with the menace of a tough, no nonsense matriarch. Men would tremble before her, and she treated them with unreserved contempt. Among my mother's friends, she had a reputation as a religious scholar, holding weekly religious classes for women in her house. Once a week she would visit all the households of the neighbourhood, taking tea and reading the riot act to deviating husbands and neglectful fathers.

My first encounter with Auntie Rashida was a memorable one. One night, on returning exhausted from a conference of Muslim students, I brought a young woman home. It was long past midnight, the lights were off, and everyone was asleep by the time we reached the door of our flat. I had forgotten my key and so had to ring the doorbell. The sound reverberated around the tower block in which we lived and seemed to meet itself in unending echoes. We waited. The pregnant pause was interminable. A light went on, and my mother, affectionately known as 'Mumsey', opened the door wearing her white nightgown. I introduced my companion to Mumsey, my eyes fixed to the ground. Mumsey looked at me; Mumsey looked at her; Mumsey turned to me again. The complexion of her face slowly merged with the whiteness of the nightgown. Then she collapsed.

The following morning, I woke up late. My companion had already departed, but in her place another woman was awaiting me. Sitting next to Mumsey at the dining table was Auntie Rashida. The Inquisition had been summoned, the condemned man would not even receive tea, let alone a hearty last meal. In the ordeal to follow Auntie Rashida would be prosecutor, judge and jury, all rolled into one.

Auntie Rashida motioned for me to sit opposite her.

'It has come to my notice,' she pronounced, looking directly at me, 'that you ... Well, let's say, you have not exactly been following the Straight Path.'

'But Auntie Rashida, nothing happened,' I sputtered my innocence. 'She needed a place to stay for the night so I brought her here.'

'Do you know what the Islamic punishment for *zina* is?' she got straight to the point.

'*Zina*? What *zina*? How can you possibly accuse me of Adultery? At worst I am guilty of allowing a sister to rest her tired head upon my equally tired shoulders. What's wrong with *that*?'

'So you admit you touched her. That is only the beginning. What happened next?'

'Nothing. *Nothing* happened.'

'Islam considers *zina* not only as a great sin but also as an act that opens the gate for many other shameful acts, which destroy the basis of family life, which lead to quarrels and murders, which ruin reputations and property, and which spread physical and spiritual disease.' I could hear the rumbling roar of civilisation as we know it collapsing in rubble about me as she spoke.

'But Auntie Rashida, nothing happened.' I was shouting, *'Nothing happened'*.

'Don't shout,' Auntie Rashida replied in her usual soft tone. 'I can hear you perfectly.' She allowed a silence for the dust to settle over the wreckage of departed civilisation before continuing. 'The punishment for *zina*,' she leaned forward, raised my chin with her index finger, and looked straight into my eyes, 'for someone like you who is not married is a hundred lashes and one year's exile from home. For a married person it is one hundred lashes followed by stoning to death.'

'What is the point of giving someone a hundred lashes if they are going to be stoned to death anyway?' I muttered miserably.

'The idea behind this punishment is not that it should be given but that it should serve as deterrent, like nuclear weapons: they are there as deterrent; they maintain the balance of power. No one in their right mind would want to use nuclear weapons. And no sensible judge would actually carry out the punishment for *zina*. Indeed, it is quite impossible to prove in a Shariah court as it requires the testimonies of four reliable and pious Muslim witnesses to be given at the same time. The witnesses must have seen the guilty persons actually committing the offence.'

'So how can you accuse me without any witnesses?'

'No one is accusing of anything.' Auntie Rashida was emphatic.

I breathed for the first time in what seemed an age of the world, breathed deep like a drowning man suddenly breaking the surface of the water.

Auntie Rashida had no need to pause for breath, she was borne along by Inquisitorial fervour. 'There are various degrees of *zina*. The Prophet, may he be blessed a thousand times, said: "The adultery of legs is walking towards a woman with unlawful intention; the adultery of the hand is touching and patting a woman that is not lawful to you; and the adultery of the eyes is casting passionate glances towards a woman."' Now she paused, gathering a mighty menace about herself, drawing in the full force of prosecutorial solemnity, exhaling the majesty of the law: 'Now, you did touch *this* woman, didn't you?'

I covered my face with my palms in shame.

There was quiet, the dull, heavy laden sepulchral quiet of doom. It seemed eons before the calm, austere voice of judgement reached across the dust-filled void. 'As a punishment, I want you to read this book.' Breaking the spell Auntie Rashida rummaged in her capacious hand bag. She withdrew a book, placed it on the table, and gently pushed it towards me.

I picked up the book and read aloud. '*Bihishti Zewar—The Jewels of Paradise*—a discussion, by section, of everything that women need to know about beliefs, legal points, ethics and social behaviour, child rearing, and so on. Compiled by the Reverent Hazrat, Sun of the Scholars, Crown of the Learned, Maulana Hafiz Muhammad Ali Sahib.'

'But this book is for women,' I commented perceptively. 'What good will it do me?'

'I was given this book on my wedding day. I entered my husband's home with the Holy Qur'an in one hand and the *Bihishti Zewar* in the other. It has helped me in my spiritual development. It will help you too, provided you read it diligently,' Auntie replied with a tart edge to her voice.

The reprieved man exulted in his freedom. The reprieved man gloried in his liberation from the rack of the Inquisitorial Matriarchate. The reprieved man nursed the wounds of trauma. He did not immediately read the book either.

But Auntie Rashida was not the kind of woman, prosecutor, judge, jury, executioner or Inquisitor to let her pronouncement go that easily. She would ask, during the suddenly more frequent visits to our home, how much of the book I had read. Justice delayed, they say, is justice denied. But justice diligently pursued, persistently harried, dedicatedly enforced by the Chinese water torture of matriarchal persistence with its soft but blatantly unsubtle repetition, let me tell you, is certain, inevitable, unavoidable, a force of nature none can resist nor evade. So *Bihishti Zewar*, also translated as *Perfecting Women*, it had to be. The final drip, which fell with the murderous power of a tidal wave and swept me to compliance, came when Auntie Rashida pointedly suggested I read the book aloud to my parents—'after all', she rightly said, 'it is essentially an oral text, written to be read aloud, discussed openly, taught in groups.' Of a sudden, I began reading the book, to myself, as conspicuously and openly as I could during every waking moment, while performing every possible task and many that, in tandem, appeared humanly impossible.

II

Written at the beginning of the twentieth century, *Bihishti Zewar* is one of the most influential texts of twentieth-century Indian Muslim reform movements. It follows the classical Islamic model of *adab*—or etiquette—literature. Conventionally, such books, encyclopaedic in nature and known under the general rubric of 'Mirror for Princes', were written for kings and rulers; the best-known being Al-Ghazzali's *Book of Counsel for Kings*, written (although the authorship is disputed) by the famous twelfth-century philosopher and dealing with qualities required in kings; the character of viziers; 'the art of the pen'; and the functions of secretaries. Many of these works, such as *The Qubus Nama* (*A Mirror for Princes*) by the eleventh-century Prince of Gurgan,

Kai Ka'us ibn Iskander, also contain rules from everyday behaviour: how to speak, eat and sleep properly, how to 'take one's pleasure' with decorum, how to find a wife, marry and make love with due etiquette. Most such works begin with a statement by the author explaining himself and his reasons for writing the book. *Bihishti Zewar* begins with the statement: 'Here I, Ashraf Ali Thanawi Hanafi, contemptible and worthless as I am, declare my purpose in writing this work.' In Islamic parlance names, and the titles included in them, are a mode of communication. 'Ashraf Ali' is his real, given name. 'Thanawi' provides us with an indication of where the author comes from: when still in his mid-thirties he retired to a small rural town called Thana Bhawan in the United Provinces of India, where the book was actually written. His house became a magnet for visitors—the visits facilitated by a new railway line that passed through Thana (meaning police station) Bhawan. His faithful followers came to believe the train tracks had been laid down with the sole purpose of taking visitors to the learned scholar. By describing himself as 'contemptible and worthless', Thanawi displays, right at the beginning, the hallmark of traditional scholarship: humility. He eschews the title of 'Maulana', the conventional designation in the Indian Subcontinent for religious scholars, or 'Sheikh', the standard Arabic label for the learned members of the *ulama*. But he does describe himself as 'Hanafi', indicating his faithfulness to one of the five principal Schools of Islamic Law and the one that predominates in India; at the same time thereby dissociating himself from the rival school of reformist religious scholars, the Ahl-e Hadith, whose members reject the Schools of Law and adhere directly to the Qur'an and the traditions of the Prophet Muhammad. To read the author's opening is to be given an orientation, a route map with convenient markers of the territory contained in the following pages. What we are about to read, we have been told, is set firmly within a specific tradition.

TWO BOOKS AND AN AUNTIE

There is another appellation Maulana Thanawi might have added: Deobandi. He was an alumni of the famous madrassa in Deoband, India. The Deoband movement emerged after the 1857 Indian revolt against British imperialism. Many veterans of the uprising came to the conclusion the battle should now be fought through education. The old Islamic seminaries had all but disappeared; what was needed was a new school to revive the tradition of Islamic education and resistance. The idea of establishing a *madrassa* for teaching religious subjects was that of a well-known Sufi saint: Haji Muhammad Abid, who lived ninety miles northeast of Delhi, in Deoband, and was to be the honorary patron of the seminary. On 14 April, 1866, when enough funding had been collected, Darul-Uloom (The House of Knowledge) Deoband was established under a pomegranate tree. The school attracted eminent teachers, many continuing their struggle against the British through warfare. Soon, Deoband acquired a reputation as a reformist institution that actively resisted British imperialism. Maulana Thanawi was from the second generation of Deobandi scholars—his anti-imperialist credentials were well established.

As I perused *Bihishti Zewar*, I found, immediately following his self-description, Maulana Thanawi's declaration of reasons for writing the book:

> For many years, I watched the ruination of the religion of the women of India and was heartbroken because of it. I struggled to find a cure, worried because that ruin was not limited to religion but had spread beyond to everyday matters as well. It went beyond the women to their children and in many respects even had its effects on their husbands. To judge from the speed with which it progressed, it seemed that if reform did not come soon, the disease would be nearly incurable. Thus I was ever more concerned.

> Thanks to divinely granted insight, experience, logic and learning, I realised that the cause of ruination is nothing other than women's

ignorance of the religious sciences. This lack corrupts their beliefs, their deeds, their dealings with other people, their character, and the whole manner of their social life. Their faith is barely spared, for they speak many words and commit many deeds that verge on infidelity ... their faulty beliefs lead to faulty character, faulty character leads to faulty action, and faulty action to faulty dealings that are the roots of anxiety in our society.

This concern, I found, led Maulana Thanawi to produce an encyclopaedic, self-help manual for paradise. *Bihishti Zewar* contains almost all a traditional Muslim woman should know: from the alphabet to advice on letter writing; from how to talk, to how to walk and lay down; from hints for household work to the correct pronunciation of Urdu words; from the stories of Prophets and Saints to the fundamental beliefs of Islam; from customs deemed sinful to customs considered legitimate; from how to get married, have sex, bring up children, to how to behave properly. The book, full of quotations from the Qur'an and the traditions of the Prophet, is crammed with lists of dos and don'ts. Not surprisingly, a great deal of the advice found in *Bihishti Zewar* is of a universal nature and eminently sensible, such as:

Do not oppress anyone.
It is very bad to tease an animal or to beat a cat or a dog.
Act respectfully before your elders.
Treat those younger than you with love and affection.
Consider no one contemptible.
Regard yourself as less than everyone else.
It is a great sin to make fun of others.
Whatever you say, say the truth.

A great deal of the material is gleaned from the classic books of etiquette, such as Maulana Thanawi's advice on how to behave in company:

TWO BOOKS AND AN AUNTIE

No one should sit in the place of a person who gets up from a gathering to do something and is expected to return. That place is hers by right.

Do not sit between two women who are deliberately sitting together in a gathering. Of course, there is no harm if they invite you to join them.

Do not act as if you are in charge of a gathering. Sit down whenever there is a space, just as the poor would do.

If you have to sneeze, cover your mouth with a cloth or with your hand, and sneeze quietly.

Stifle a yawn as best you can. If you cannot, at least cover your mouth.

Do not laugh loudly.

In a gathering, do not extend your feet in anyone's direction.

On the subject of how to eat and drink:

Say 'Bi'smi'llah' (In the name of God) before eating. Eat with your right hand. Eat from the side of the dish nearest you. If several kinds of things are served, such as several kinds of fruits or sweets, you may choose whatever you like and eat what your heart desires.

Take melon slices, dates, grapes, or sweets one at a time. Do not take two at a time.

When you eat something such as raw onions or garlic, rinse out your mouth to get rid of the smell if you are going to sit in company.

Be considerate of a guest. If you in turn are a guest, do not stay so long that you begin to burden your host.

And, on the subject of dealing with other people:

Do not squander the money God gives you. Refrain from spending money unless there is a genuine necessity.

People who are forced to sell their goods in distress should be considered people in need. Do not take advantage of them. Do not force them to lower their price. Either help them or buy their things at a suitable price.

Do not harass poor debtors. Either give them extra time or remit part or all of their debt.

It is wrong to refuse a request to repay a debt if you have the means to pay.

Much of this advice is freely mixed with Indian Muslim folk-lore: 'If you have a frightening dream, spit three times to the left and repeat three times: "I seek refuge in God from Satan, the Cursed," then turn over and mention the dream to no one. If someone is suspected of casting an evil eye wash her face, both arms up to the elbows, both feet, both knees, and her private parts. Collect the water and pour it over the head of the person afflicted, and, Almighty God Willing, that person will be cured.'

In proof that I was not only a reprieved man but one diligently observing his repentance by fulfilling the entire letter and spirit of his remedial punishment, I once addressed my father according to the prescription in *Bihishti Zewar*: 'Respected father, sir, the *qibla* and Kaaba of your descendants, the object of service from your dependents, may your lofty shadow never vanish. After salutation with endless respects and exaltation, I beg to submit ...' It was not a success.

In similar vein, I found it easy, at the outset, to dismiss *Bihishti Zewar* as an archaic, conservative book—another formula for punctilious observance of prescribed duties, taking its readers to paradise by numbers. But the more I read the more paradoxical it became. Gradually, it became clear to me this was not a traditional but a modernist text. Traditionally, women are not seen, addressed nor included in the mainstream of Islamic teaching, but *Bihishti Zewar* insists women should know what has traditionally been the preserve of men in mosques, courts, schools, and Sufi groups. There could be only one conclusion, that it was meant as an instrument of cultural transformation. Moreover, despite the fact it is clearly addressed to women, the teachings are aimed at all. The aim is to instil a reformist disposition based on moderation in all things, modesty in all aspects of life, and strict self-control in all spheres. The inscrutability of Auntie Rashida's judgement and her intransigent insistence that I read this book were starting to make sense.

At the end of *Bihishti Zewar*, the learned Maulana thoughtfully provides a list of 'forbidden books'. It includes well-known texts such as the *Thousand and One Nights* and the *Tales of Amir Hamza*, and all books of poetry. When I came to this passage I recoiled. Historically, the Inquisition had led to the Index, the list of forbidden books, but it had never occurred to me Auntie Rashida might be that kind of Inquisition. I read the list over and over again, becoming more and more perplexed. Something, suddenly, was not at all right. Something did not fit, let alone make sense. Whatever worthy instruction I might gather along the way, how could Auntie Rashida have led me to this denouement? Was not Auntie Rashida herself a great devotee of Urdu poetry—as indeed were my parents? Did she herself not devour Urdu novels, including those on the forbidden list? Had I not seen many of these forbidden texts on Auntie Rashida's bookshelf? After her tidal wave of judicial urgings, it seemed, she was leaving me marooned amidst mixed messages, more perplexed than ever. What, exactly, was she trying to tell me?

The question intrigued me. More than that, it became an obsession. This most imperfect culmination to the perfection of women was a hellish problem I kept turning over in my mind in search of some resolution. Unable to satisfy myself, I determined to resort to intrigue. One day, when I knew Auntie Rashida was out addressing a women's meeting, I decided to visit her house. Her husband was home; indeed, he was always home—some strange illness had led him to give up his teaching job and confined him to a rather cushy armchair. I made some excuse, poured him a cup of tea, and began to browse the bookshelf. Yes: Auntie Rashida had been reading all those books Maulana Thanawi had explicitly forbidden. One in particular had been thumbed numerous times: page after page underlined, annotations in the margins, passages flanked by mathematical signs. I interpreted an √ sign to mean Aunty Rashida agreed with the passage; ∫ indicated she was trying to integrate the passage with what she already knew; and Σ signified she was trying to summarise the arguments. What was the meaning of this calculus? Was this the key to explaining the nature of the judgement she had laid upon me. What I held in my hand was no instructional manual; it was a novel. I tucked the book under my jacket and slipped out of her house.

III

Mirat ul-Arus—The Bride's Mirror—is claimed by many to be the first Urdu novel; it was certainly the first Urdu best-seller. Published in 1869, almost half a century before *Bihishti Zewar*, it is the story of two sisters: Akbari (Big) and Asghari (Small). Akbari is bad tempered, uneducated, not very pious and, in the final analysis, a failure. Asghari is literate, competent, pious, patient and finally successful both in this life and the Hereafter; a fictional representation of the perfect women *Bihishti Zewar* aims to produce. It is, as its author Nazir Ahmad suggested, a syllabus, in the narrative form, for the instruction of women.

So why would Maulana Thanawi forbid *Mirat ul-Arus*?

Like Maulana Thanawi, Nazir Ahmad was deeply religious, with a distinguished religious ancestry. He learned Arabic and Persian from his father and studied at the Aurangabadi Mosque in Delhi. Later, he attended the Delhi College to learn Urdu, because his father had told him that 'he would rather see me die than learn English'. He joined the British colonial administration, probably causing much anguish to his father, became a deputy inspector of schools and went on to serve as Deputy Collector in the Revenue Service. Often referred to as 'Deputy' Nazir Ahmad, he also wrote what many considered to be one of the finest novels of Urdu literature: *Tabahtun Nisa* (*The Repentance of Women*), which is set in Delhi at a time when an epidemic of plague was raging. I read it, with great empathy, while studying for my Urdu 'O' level. Like a detective forensically piecing together the elements of a crime, I began to consider possible motives for the Maulana's disapproval of the Deputy. Clearly, it could have something to do with the fact he has seen Nazir Ahmad as colluding with the Christian English to the detriment of Muslim Indians. The fact Nazir Ahmad equated Islam with other religions would also have been problematic for the Maulana. His mockery of certain religious figures, like the Maulana himself, could not have helped matters either. But these reasons, in themselves, simply did not convince as a sufficiently compelling motive for *Mirat ul-Arus* to end up on the forbidden list of *Bihishti Zewar*. Whatever their differences, both men reached the same conclusion and were allied in proposing that it was women who would eventually usher in Islamic reform: paradise, after all, as Prophet Muhammad said, lies under the feet of mothers.

Yet there is a crucial parting of the ways. Fitting the evidence together, I at last found the crux of the matter. For all that women were the means to true reform, the gatekeepers of paradise, it was the realm and sphere of their activity that so completely divided the two works. Maulana Thanawi was determined that women be confined within the walls of the family home; Nazir Ahmad wished to liberate them. Maulana's women are independent but docile, deferring to men; Ahmad's women are capable, dynamic and tower over the men in the novel. And this led on to the ultimate heresy, the idea that women could be better than men. Here was the clear anathema for Maulana Thanawi.

A PERSON OF PAKISTANI ORIGINS

In Islam, Nazir Ahmad writes in the introduction to the novel, there is no distinction between men and women. Women have the same faculties as men and can become as learned and famous. Moreover, this is a seminal point in the structure of the message of Islam, one mouthed but seldom acknowledged, mouthed only to be significantly and emphatically neglected. The Qu'ran explicitly and repeatedly addresses itself to 'the believing men and the believing women', 'the believing women and the believing men'. This form of address is used whenever the Qu'ran commends a specific operative principle, an aspect of its moral and ethical framework to be enacted by the community. But, when we look at 'the common practice' we discover that 'no value is set upon women', as the Deputy wrote. Indeed, the practice is deeply entrenched: 'public opinion and the custom of the country have made a retired life behind the purdah obligatory and incumbent upon women, and in these days the observance of this institution is more rigid than ever,' he writes. His novel serves to elaborate and reflect upon the social consequences. Strict observance of religious ritual as conventionally understood becomes not merely a regimen, but in practice a prison; by the very act of following this routine of strict observance, a pattern of life and thought is established that denies the very essence of the message. What was true in the time of the Deputy remains in force in many Muslim societies, continuing to be internalised as the 'real' ideal by those of a pious, observant persuasion. It is not only a matter of men believing women should be confined, even if they are to be educated in their confinement. The very worst of the matter is the millions upon millions of Muslim women, educated or not, who have internalised this idea, who observantly and scrupulously imprint this ideal on their children by indulging and pampering their sons, inculcating the double standards that are to last a lifetime, fostering the restrictions that confine the outlook, ambition and destiny of their daughters and ensuring this way of being passes down the generations as the ultimate recessive gene. How could the Deputy not be correct? The marginalisation of one half of the entire Muslim community more than halved the possibility of vibrant revitalisation. If the basic institution of the Muslim world, the family, was deformed by this engendered imbalance, then all other institutions would be affected: neighbourhood, community, society, nations as a whole were part of the ramifying chain reaction, distorted in its wake. The most educated, most observant, most pious women were the most punctilious in teaching their children the manners, morals and ethos of Islam in its gender truncated variant of limited female aspiration. To change the circumstances and mind-set of women, therefore, would be a fundamental shift. It would energise the remodelling of the entire fabric and structure of Muslim existence then, now or at any time in the future. Nazir Ahmed's pertinent question was, sadly, timeless: with the route to reform confined 'while living in purdah, how are you to acquire' the capacity to transcend your boundaries? He proposed the only possible answer, education—but not the kind of 'bad education' one finds in *Bihishti Zewar*. Instead, the Deputy's argument that women must seek real education suggests his preferred answer lies in the kind of education that promotes knowledge: women must seek learning. With that the Deputy is off towards a new trajectory: 'And now I am going to tell you an amusing story, which will show you what kind of troubles are brought about by a bad education.'

In the novel, the badly educated Akbari is a model of how to do everything wrong. Asghari is a much more rounded and complex character. She transforms her father and discreetly takes over the affairs of her father-in-law and brother-in law while building the career of her husband, Muhammad Kamil. She encourages him to accept a modest apprenticeship at the courts then move to a slightly better post while looking out for a better one. God's will alone, she tells him, will not get him a better position: nothing can be gained without his own efforts. When he begins to meander from the path of virtue, she travels alone to a remote place, compels his bad companions to flee, and reshapes his life to her own virtuous specifications. In the conclusion of the novel, we discover Asghari has left quite a legacy behind: 'the things which she achieved under these conditions— for all that she was a woman—will no doubt remain in the world as memorials of her to the last day; but unfortunately I have not the leisure to set them down in writing.' But we know that she has left a mansion, a mosque, a caravanserai, and a number of charitable trusts in Delhi. Despite all this, Asghari, in my view, is problematic: she cannot totally free herself from men, constantly consulting her father and her father-in-law. Nazir Ahmad too had his limitations—the nineteenth-century world in which he was writing.

IV

A few days after I had purloined *Mirat ul-Arus*, Auntie Rashida cornered me.

'Young man,' she said in her usual soft tone, 'when exactly did you decide to become a thief?'

'When I saw a copy of *Mirat ul-Arus* on your bookshelf.'

'Islam permits the theft of books,' she acknowledged with a smile.

'Why did you not give me *Mirat ul-Arus* straight away to read?' I asked.

'Because, without reading *Bihishti Zewar* you could not really appreciate *Mirat ul-Arus*. Both books are concerned with perfection and aim to reform Muslim societies. Both are problematic. But together they suggest the same sources can give rise to totally different ideas on reform.' Auntie Rashida paused. Her smile evaporated slowly and she became rather solemn. 'I am too set in my old ways,' she said. 'But we all look to young people like you to come up with more meaningful notions of reform.' She looked straight into my eyes. 'Now go out,' she said with some determination, 'and reinvent tradition'.

I have been following Auntie Rashida's orders ever since.

4.

••••••••

DILIP KUMAR
MADE ME DO IT

••••••••

I

On my twelfth birthday, I was burdened with two responsibilities: one was a chore, the other a pleasure. In the early sixties,
the British Asian community was still in an embryonic stage of
development. In Hackney, my part of East London, there were
neither halal meat shops nor cinemas that showed Indian films.
So every Saturday afternoon, I took a bus to Aldgate East to buy
the weekly supply of halal meat. On Sundays, I took my mother
to either the Cameo Theatre in Walthamstow or the Scala at
Kings Cross to see 'two films on one ticket'.

The weekly visit to the cinema was a full day affair. My mother
would start her preparation for the ritual early in the morning.
The latest issue of the Urdu weekly *Mashriq* (now defunct)
would be scanned to discover the current offering at our regular
theatres. Should we opt for the latest Dilip Kumar double bill at
the Cameo or see Guru Dutt's *Payisa* once again at the Scala?
The decision was never an easy one, but the strategy followed by
my mother was always the same. First, she would try and coax
my father both to join in the outing and take a lead in making
the decision. This ploy seldom worked. Next, Mrs Mital and Mrs
Hassan, the Asian families of the neighbourhood, would be con-
sulted. Intense discussion would follow on the merits of the
offerings, minds and positions would change frequently, before a
consensus was reached. We would leave for the cinema at around
twelve, my mother carrying a bag laden with sandwiches, stuffed
prathas, drinks and a generous supply of tissues. Sometimes Mrs
Mital, or Mrs Hassan, or both, would be in tow. The long wait

for the bus, often in bitterly cold or relentlessly rainy conditions, would be rewarded by an equally long wait to get inside the cinema. I would queue for the tickets while my mother and our neighbours would eagerly look around for faces they could recognise. They had made numerous friends during these weekly excursions; friends whom they saw only at the cinema and chatted to only during the intervals. I would always return from the ticket office to discover that my mother had bumped into a veritable horde of friends and that they all wanted to sit together. The logistics of finding the appropriate seating pattern in the midst of hundreds of similar networks with identical aspirations would have truly taxed the ability of a beach master at the Normandy landings. The performance started promptly at two o'clock and while my mother and her friends watched the films with rapt attention, most of the men in the audience would participate in each film, expostulating vociferously with hoots or hisses as circumstances demanded. During memorable dance sequences, notably those involving Helen, the participants would hurl money at the screen. And like a throbbing tidal undertow to the film's dialogue and music, and breaking through the hubbub of the audience, would rise and fall the inconsolable heart-wrenching gasps of sobbing women. In the midst of all this I would intersperse avidly watching the film with servicing my mother, Mrs Mital and Mrs Hassan with a generous supply of tissues to staunch their unending tears. We would leave the cinema somewhere after eight-thirty in the evening, exhausted, emotionally drained but thoroughly entertained.

Yet all this was only the prelude, the day was far from over. On her return, my mother would insist on telling the stories of both films to my father. His protests would have no effect on her; locking himself in the bathroom was ineffectual; stuffing his fingers in his ears brought no relief: she just would not rest until she had related the narratives of the films in all possible detail. Then came the moment we all cherished: once she had the narrative off her chest, my mother would move on to the songs. She would hum the lyrics to us, taking great pleasure in reiterating the poetic imagery of the songs. At this point, my father would forget that he was tired, that he loathed films, and would sit up at full attention. 'Wah, wah,' he would exclaim. 'Repeat the first verse.' 'Umm! The second verse does not do justice to the first.' This would go on for a while before my father would jump up in excitement and declare that the first verse would become the basis of our next *mushaira*.

Now, it was a custom of my family to hold a *mushaira*—poetry recital—on the last Saturday of every month. These were late night, all-night affairs. My father would select the opening verse of a film song and the invited participants would have to justify their inclusion in the gathering by writing a full *ghazal* based on this opening verse. He would insist that everyone recited their *ghazal* in *taranum*—that is, actually sang their *ghazal* as though it was a film song; although my father's own *taranum* left a considerable amount to be desired. After dutifully preparing the meals for these occasions, my mother would sit up praising, criticising and eventually, in an effortless but novel twist, performing her own *ghazal*. I remember being a full participant in these mushairas and writing a few *ghazals* myself.

But Indian films did not only set the literary agenda in our house. Through my mother's constant reiteration of film narratives, they also established our social and intellectual priorities. For us, Indian cinema was just that: Indian in a true multicultural sense. There were no divisions here between 'Muslims', 'Hindus', 'Sikhs' or 'Pakistanis' and 'Indians': all of us identified with the characters and found meaning in the narratives. The films testified to the fact that all were culturally and socially one. We saw them as a universal symbol of our subcontinental identity; a lifeline for the cultural survival of the Asian community. They brought a little bit of 'home', of what my parents had left behind in Pakistan, to us here in Britain and thus provided a sense of belonging not offered by British society. But, more than that, they also conveyed the problems of the society we had left behind. Problems that my parents were convinced would not be repeated here; would have no place in the emerging Asian community of Britain. By her constant, undaunted retelling of film stories, my mother made the deep social and economic inequalities of subcontinental society, the inferior position of women, the conflict between tradition and modernity, topics of everyday discussion. On reflection, it seems to me now that she brought more than film characters alive: my own consciousness was not so much dazzled by celluloid heroes and heroines, it was stretched by the three dimensional cultural, social and intellectual ideas and issues they personified.

Our house was a microcosm of the Asian community as a whole. Asian Britain was incorporated by the social institution of Indian cinema in which it had a double emotional investment. Firstly, as a prime cultural referent Indian films reflected the diversity and density of life 'back home' and provided a direct emotional link with the Subcontinent. Secondly, it furnished a subconscious agenda for the future: problems to be avoided, social issues to be addressed, cultural goals to be sought, ideological possibilities to be explored through the empowerment of being migrants in Britain. Indian films were thus much more than entertainment: they were a source of contemplation as well as a reservoir of aesthetic and cultural values. They brought different elements of the community together and through this adhesive offered the prospect of rising above the dilemmas the Subcontinent had not resolved.

II

On my thirtieth birthday, I joined London Weekend Television (LWT) to work as a reporter on a pioneering new programme for the Asian community. This was immediately after a new television network, Channel 4, had been established with a special mandate to serve the needs of minorities within the convention of British television. Prior to the emergence of Channel 4, the needs of the Asian audience were seen mainly in terms of remedial education. For well over a decade, BBC's 'Nai Zindigi, Nai Jewan' programme treated the Asian audiences as infants suffering from serious educational impediments. LWT's 'Eastern Eye', broadcast fortnightly on Channel 4, changed all that. The hour-long magazine programme became a trendsetter in the way a team of Asian reporters handled Asian stories and brought many Asian faces to the mainstream of British television. By far the most popular strand of the programme was the one dealing with Indian films. Apart from star interviews and a film quiz, this involved showing clips from the latest films, often accompanied with sardonic comments.

I frequently found myself handling the film sections of the programme: this involved both choosing the clips to be shown and writing the studio scripts that introduced, linked and commented on them. Both the new films that were coming our way and the response from 'Eastern Eye' viewers convinced me that Indian films and their British Asian audience had changed profoundly. The film narrative, as the prime instance and instrument of contemplation and self-reflection, had evaporated. Film songs were no longer *ghazals* written by reputable poets, but meaningless words strung together to the beat of a disco number. The audience themselves were not interested in the narrative but only wanted to see disco dances and fight scenes. Moreover, they were not willing to entertain any critical, particularly sardonic comments, either about the films or their stars: the viewers demanded total respect and awe. Films were engendering not *mushairas* in Asian households, as they did during my youth, it was the stylised and patently absurd fight scenes that were being enacted throughout the Asian community. Far from resisting their status as commodity—as did the earlier films by means of stylistic self-reference—the new films projected themselves solely as what they were: commercial vehicles for one-dimensional celluloid characters. The aesthetic experience that stressed contemplation had given way to mindless action.

As an 'Eastern Eye' reporter, I travelled throughout Britain hunting for stories, investigating criminals, exposing racism. I was thus able to visit countless Asian households all across the country. In each Asian home the story was largely the same: whatever the condition of the house and the financial status of the occupant, the video player would be on and the parents would be huddled together with their children watching Indian movies. There would always be a pile of rented films next to the television. Three or four films a day would be the normal fare. Often I would enter a home to interview the parents and discover the children were fast-forwarding the video to savour the fight scenes or disco dances that they then played in slow motion. When they were not watching, they were enacting fight scenes, uttering incomprehensibly aggressive dialogues, or swinging like their favourite hero or heroine. In the youth clubs I visited and social gatherings I attended, the accent was on emulating Amitabh Bachchan or Shabana Azmi. Young men and women took great care in practising their dance routines, often rehearsing in front of the mirror in the toilets in preparation for launching themselves, suitably clad, onto the hub of the social life of the new Asian British community.

For these new consumers, the source of pleasure in Indian movies was not the identification of characters or situations, the language or the poetic imagery (if any), but solely the extent of the aggression shown by the hero and the manner and content of the violence he was able to dole out to the villains along with the style and spectacle of disco dances. These were not the Indian films of my childhood; and these audiences were certainly not the kind of movie goers with which I, my mother and her numerous friends, shared the confines of the Walthamstow Cameo or Kings Cross Scala to watch Dilip Kumar or Guru Dutt unfold the contradictions and problems, injustices and social malaise, poetry and aesthetics, richness and diversity of Indian culture.

III

On my fifteenth birthday I saw *Mughal-e-Azam*. I remember it well: it was one of those rare occasions when my father accompanied us to the Walthamstow Cameo. But there are other reasons why the memory of my first exposure to *Mughal-e-Azam* is so vividly engrained in my mind. It was the only film to be shown on its own: every time it was screened, the 'two films on one ticket' philosophy went out of the window. It is a rare film in that it does not have the stock-in-trade of all Indian films: a comedian. No one laughed during its screening; indeed no one hissed, or hooted, or even moved, though everyone cried. We did not so much watch *Mughal-e-Azam* as immersed ourselves in it. But above all, I remember *Mughal-e-Azam* because it taught me the critical, linguistic and visual, appreciation of the *ghazal*: it was my object lesson in the meaning of poetry.

Mughal-e-Azam was one of the five main texts of my youth— and its star, Dilip Kumar, was my guide and pathfinder. He was not my 'hero': both his films, as well as the eclectic analysis of their narratives by my mother, would never have allowed an impressionable young man to simply accept Dilip Kumar as an object of adoration for unquestioning hero worship. No. He was my guide through the complex world of human emotions; he opened certain paths and invited me to journey through them, to examine and cross-examine what I discovered en route, to dissect and analyse what I encountered. Along with *Mughal-e-Azam*,

Devdas and *Gunga Jumna* were my other Dilip Kumar texts. But he could not be my hero for another reason: I was equally drawn towards Guru Dutt. Whereas Dilip Kumar took me to the edge of emotional intensity, Guru Dutt opened my eyes to the reality of the world. One Muslim, one Hindu—yet their different faiths impressed themselves upon me for the synthesis they made possible. What they expressed were discrete outlooks that were part of a necessary dialogue, one stretching the other, tempering the other, informing the other, each enriched, each part of a cultural synthesis, each at home in India: my India. Hence making it possible for me to deal with Britain.

The Muslim and Hindu dimensions of India—the culture, the civilisation, the people—fuse together in a seamless whole in K. Asif's *Mughal-e-Azam*. The narrative concerns the love affair of the Mughal Prince Salim, played by Dilip Kumar, and the courtier Anarkali. Between the lovers stands Salim's father, the mighty Mughal emperor Akbar, his Hindu mother, the Queen of Jodha, the scheming courtier, Bahar, who harbours the secret desire to become the Queen and is herself vying for Salim's attentions, and the social conventions of Mughal India. For Salim, love is far above royal protocol and conventions; for Akbar and the Queen, social convention is everything, although Akbar is also plagued with his own ambiguous ideas of absolute justice. Anarkali knows that her love is pitting father against son and the outcome can only be tragic. Bahar is determined to usher in the tragedy. While allegedly based on a true historical incident, the film makes no attempt to be historically accurate. Indeed, its narrative is deliberately couched in myth and metaphor to link the past with the present: the tragedy that was once played out in the court of Akbar is universal, it is unfolding in every Indian community. We are invited to read Mughal social conventions as the social institutions and class structure of modern day India.

Moghal-e-Azam is structured like a *ghazal*. Before the advent of the film, the Urdu *ghazal* was the main source of cultural expression and cultural entertainment in urban India, as depicted, so charmingly, in Kamal Amrohi's *Pakeeza*. Essentially, the *ghazal* consists of love lyrics with fixed metrical form which can easily be rendered into music. While love is its prime theme, a *ghazal* need not be solely about love: a good *ghazal* wraps a great deal of philosophy, metaphysics, social comment and symbolism into its metaphors, similies and basic theme. Each couplet in a *ghazal* is capable of standing on its own, it may not even bear a direct subject relationship to the previous one, but the whole *ghazal* has a thematic unity and psychic continuity. The symbolic and metaphoric content of a *ghazal* makes it particularly amenable to visualisation.

The characters of *Mughal-e-Azam* do not just speak: they refine communication, they distil it, they crystallise it into many faceted glittering gems, they make poetry of ordinary language. When Bahar asks Prince Salim to accompany her on some routine task, she says:

> Eyes long to glimpse at you,
> Paths await your shadow!

When Salim discovers that Bahar has been spying on him and Anarkali, he summons her to his chambers. She enters the chamber to discover him standing by a candle:

> Salim: What does a candle flame know?
> Bahar: Murmurs of the night and a few secrets.
> Salim: For that reason every candle-flame is extinguished at break of day. You tried to know a secret; you too can be extinguished.

When the film is not encasing dialogue in symbolism and metaphor, it simply erupts into verse. Salim's declaration of love comes in the form of a poem to Anarkali; Anarkali replies in verse. The two lovers even arrange their meeting place via poetry. Determined to settle her differences with Anarkali, Bahar invites her to a poetic duel, which she wins. The total immersion of

Indian culture in Urdu poetry is truly brought home when Anarkali feels the need to consult an oracle. She closes her eyes and simply opens a Diwan (an anthology of poems) and reads the first verse that catches her eye!

The film's structure moves from narrative point to narrative point with the same poetic intensity. Each sequence is a synoptic expression of the theme, the whole story prefigured in each episode of its narrative unfolding.

The opening sections of the film establish that we are being invited to a meditation on love and beauty, art and life. On his return from battle, Prince Salim sees a veiled statue and learns of the bold claims of the sculptor: his art transcends life, it can subdue warriors, dethrone kings, make ordinary men give up life. Salim wants to see the sculpture but the courtiers prevent him, warning that the royal astrologer has cautioned that seeing the statue before the moon sets could spell disaster, and that the King has ordered the unveiling at dawn in his presence. Unable to contain his curiosity, Salim returns in the middle of the night. As he looks through the beaded curtain of pearls, he declares: 'The sculptor's claim is indeed justified. Only marble can endure the intensity of such infinite beauty. I am tempted to accept the divinity of idols.' His faithful assistant and companion, Darjan warns: 'You will be accused of idolatry.' Salim quips: 'But praised for my devotion to beauty.' As Salim walks away from the sculpture, we discover Bahar has been watching him violate the order of the king, and hear the following off-screen dialogue:

> Voice: I could not complete the statue. You must stand in its place tomorrow.
>
> Anarkali: The Prince has seen me; he praised your art.

The following morning the statue is unveiled in front of Akbar the Great. Bahar suggests that the conventions of romantic literature should be followed and the sculpture should be unveiled with an arrow. In accepting her suggestion the King comments that stories have a habit of turning into reality. Salim shoots the arrow; the sculpture is unveiled. Akbar exclaims: 'Praise be to Allah! It seems an angel has descended from heaven and taken form in marble.' Then the statue moves and bows:

Anarkali: I am no angel but a human being.

Akbar: Then who forced you to become a statue.

Anarkali: A wilful sculptor of your realm whose name no one knows.

Akbar: His art is indeed praiseworthy. But why did you remain silent when the arrow was shot?

Anarkali: I wanted to see how romantic fiction is transformed into reality.

And like reality the film is many-layered and complex. Not just the reality that Salim, Akbar and Anarkali are actual historic characters with legendary status, but the social reality of India where status, class and creed are a constant barrier to the realisation of genuine love. We know that, as the narrative unfolds, several arrows will be shot at Anarkali, not least by Salim himself; Salim will constantly challenge Akbar's orders; and Akbar—not Salim—will be tempted to accept the divinity of idols: his own power, Mughal social customs, and his awkward notion of 'justice'. For Akbar, Anarkali will always be a statue—to be admired from a distance, unframed, and, if necessary, destroyed. For Salim, she is not only the object of love but of total surrender. And before the narrative ends, Anarkali herself will not only live out the conventions of romantic literature but will actually establish them.

As the narrative moves, each section rekindles the theme of the statue and the connection between life and art—just as a *ghazal* would repeat its symbolic idea. When Salim accuses Anarkali of 'false love' he recasts her in wax: you are like a wax sculpture and, as such, have no genuine emotions, he says. We discover that the sculptor had no real intention of making a statue; for him, Anarkali was living art—her love for Salim, he predicted, would unfold as a work of sublime art. When Akbar sends Salim to be executed, the sculptor accuses him of being a statue of granite and sings:

> He whose religion is royal splendour
> Is a man without creed;
> He whose heart is devoid of love
> Is formed of granite, not flesh!

Art and life are two sides of the same coin; art cannot be divorced from life. This intimate connection is emphasised in the film's songs and dances. In the Indian cinema of the fifties, sixties and early seventies, song and dance are an integral part of the narrative. In Mughal-e-Azam, they are used both to make narrative points and to move the story forward. The intensity of these sequences is heightened by another major stylistic tour de force: the switch from black and white, in which the rest of the film is shot, to technicolour. In the film's most famous song and dance sequence, Anarkali makes a number of important narrative points as colour bleeds into the screen:

> When one has loved why should one be afraid?
> I am only in love, I am not a thief.
> I shall tell the story of my love
> Let the world take my life...

Not only does Anarkali tell Salim, who has accused her of playing with his emotions, that her love is true but also that she is ready to sacrifice everything for her love. She also declares her defiance of Akbar, reveals her love for Salim to the Queen—indeed, makes a public pronouncement:

> Our love cannot be concealed
> It is there for all to see

Akbar sees her reflection everywhere—in the chandeliers and glass decorations of the palace, multiplied thousands of times. As the song ends, the dance concludes, and Akbar, in an uncontrol-lable rage, rises from his throne. Off camera we hear an almighty crash—the statue has finally shattered and a living individual, with all her emotions and aspirations, has emerged.

In the film's other colour sequence, the song is used to sum up the narrative. Akbar has granted Anarkali one night with Salim on the condition that she drugs him before dawn and surrenders herself to be executed immediately. In their only and final night together, the lovers are entertained by Bahar, who is aware of the plan. She is taunting Anarkali but knows that in Anarkali's defeat and final erasure, there is a much greater victory:

How can heart pine less?
How can love diminish?
When the night is so drunken
What shall dawn be like?
The melodies are intoxicating
Goblets brim with joy
The joy that reigns here will be
The romantic literature of tomorrow.
Within this splendour why should
Anyone give a thought to death?

The lovers are ecstatic in each other's company, there is no dialogue between them. Indeed, on most occasions when Anarkali and Salim are together they look at each other in medi-tative silence. When, earlier in the film, Anarkali meets Salim, she passes by the famous Mughal musician Tan Sain engaged in his regular evening rehearsal. The lovers' meditative silence is realised by the intervals in Tan Sain's music: the duration of the intervals produce tonal and auditory tension captured in the glances exchanged by the lovers. The purity of the musical notes resonates with the purity of Anarkali and Salim's love for each other. It is not just the connection between love and music that is being played here. Just as music conveys deep mystical meaning, so the ecstasy of love is realised not in a physical but a spiritual union.

The notion that love is spiritual and not merely physical is crucial not just to understanding *Mughal-e-Azam* but Indian culture itself. Mysticism is a central feature of both Islam and Hinduism: in their unconditional love of God, the mystics seek total annihilation of their Self in the Divine. Since both Islam and Hinduism see the physical and spiritual as an integrated whole, it is natural for Indian culture to postulate that true love, love worthy of serious consideration, must move from physical to spiritual realms: the lovers must unconditionally surrender themselves to each other without concern for worldly consequences. Only in following in the footsteps of the mystics can the lovers elevate their initial physical attraction to a new level of consciousness and spiritual union. This is the message of such classics of romantic literature as *Laila Majnu, Heer Ranja, Shreen Farhad* and Sarat Chandra Chatterjee's popular Bengali novel, *Devdas*, which was originally made into a film by P. C. Barua in 1935 and remade, with Dilip Kumar in the lead, in 1955.

Devdas, the son of a wealthy landowner, falls in love with Parvati, the daughter of a poor man he has known since childhood. When Devdas is away studying in Calcatta, Parvati's father arranges her marriage to an elderly man. Despite her love for Devdas, Parvati decides to suffer in silence and obey her father. When Devdas hears the news, he is heart-broken and takes to drink. He is befriended by Chandra, a prostitute, who is totally devoted to him and is willing to give up everything to save him. Parvati too tries to save Devdas without much success. The drink takes it toll, Devdas becomes ill and finally dies outside Parvati's house.

Devdas has been much criticised for presenting, in the words of Kishore Valicha, 'a deeply pessimistic view of human relations, of love and of life, an unmitigated philosophy of despair'. But to criticise the purity of Devdas's love as 'a love devoid of any sexual significance' is to totally miss the point. Devdas's love for Parvati, as that of Salim for Anarkali, is unconditional: Parvati is not the object of his love but the subject of his total surrender. To see Devdas as a pessimist, self-pitying and self-destructive lover is to reduce him to a single dimension, a categorisation that his complex character singularly refuses to accept. He never says what he means, and his words always convey the opposite meaning to his true intensions. He is an idealist seeking the impossible: the release of his suffering, which could only be achieved by raising his love for Parvati to a more sublime and spiritually unified state. His long and tortuous, apparently meaningless, train journey is, in fact, a metaphor for his personal quest for a spiritual union with Parvati: a mystical journey at the end of which lies the total dissolution of the Self. The climax of the film, the burning of Devdas's body on the funeral pyre, signifies the ultimate release from his suffering. For Devdas, this is the only apotheosis of the irreconcilable challenge of his love in an actual social and cultural environment. In this ending the audience finds a beginning, a challenge to reflection and action.

The theme of Devdas is consciously reiterated by Guru Dutt in *Kaagaz Ke Phool* (1959)—'Paper Flowers'—to provide us with another complex reflection on impossibilities and the shadow world they create in modern India. The central character is Suresh, played by Guru Dutt, a film director engaged in making *Devdas*. So we have a film within a film whose narrative is told in flashback, another film within a film, a film where ends proceed beginnings. The many-layered story-telling in *Kaagaz ka Phool* is set amidst a comedy of manners, but the various levels of comedy are neither random nor gratuitous and are definitely not simple light relief—they are an essential dynamic driving the tragedy of human relations, which is the heart of the film. The juxtaposition makes *Kaagaz ke Phool* a discourse on filmmaking and fame as well as on tradition and modernity and the ineptness of both to generate human fulfilment in a contemporary setting. It is a bitter satire created through the rapid succession of incongruous moods.

The narrative begins after we have been told the story. An old man limps into a film studio and the overlaid song reflects on the life that has brought this visibly poor wreck to his present condition:

> *What have I gained from this world*
> *I am left with nothing but tears*
> *Once my path was strewn with flowers*
> *Now I can't even hope for thorns*
> *Selfishness drives this world*
> *I have seen many who parted ways one by one…*
> *Spring is like a guest who stays just one night*
> *When the night ends happiness fades with the dawn*
> *All happiness lasts just a fleeting moment*
> *Everywhere there is a sense of unease…*

But the opening lyrics turn out to be ironic since, the tragedy of *Kaagaz ke Phool* is the product of selflessness and the quest for selfless fulfilment. The old man remembers when he was a famous and successful film director. What he remembers is an incongruous figure, a thoughtful man in his prime, reflectively puffing on his pipe amidst the glitter and acclaim of a triumphant career; a man apart in the middle of all the adulation he receives because his big house is as empty as is his life, despite his conspicuous achievements. He has only a cupboard of old memories, symbolised by a child's doll.

In Delhi for the launch of his latest film, Suresh visits his daughter Pammi. We learn that he is separated from his wife and, as the headmistress informs him, thus denied access to his child on her mother's instructions. Suresh determines to challenge his ex-wife but cannot penetrate the indifference and heartless elegance of her exotic family: Sir B.B.Verma and his vapid wife, surrounded by their dogs and their playboy son

Rocky. This elite ménage of wealth and position is responsible for his separation first from his wife and then from his daughter. The pompous and opinionated Sir B.B. explains that his home is dedicated to fine things not vulgarity. The dirty world of film—dirty because its panders to the common populace—is a social shame to his honour and reputation; as his wife points out, Suresh's name cannot even be mentioned in their polite society. The product of all their refinement is that they lavish inappropriate attention on a bunch of dogs; their daughter hides herself away and refuses to discuss her own daughter's well-being with the husband she abandoned; and the irrepressible Rocky lives a seemingly irresponsible lifestyle owning race horses, drinking and womanising.

As he wanders aimlessly in the rain after leaving the Verma household, Suresh meets a beautiful young woman taking shelter under a tree. Decency is the subject of their witty word play: she is not the kind of girl who talks to strangers and doesn't like films; he makes films but is not the kind of man who accosts young women. She is too poor to own a coat and he leaves her his overcoat to keep her from the rain, before rushing off to catch his train to Bombay and plunge back into the world of film.

In Delhi we have seen everything Suresh wants and cannot have. In Bombay he is a lion who can have anything he desires to make his films. Even the most fashionable actress must succumb to his quest for authentic simplicity, even the studio bosses must indulge his decisions. But nothing could be less appropriate to Suresh's quest than the dramatis personae arranged by the studio. Into this farce walks Shanti, the poor girl from Delhi. Intent on returning the overcoat, she blunders onto the film set and, by a chance mistake, the wrong piece of film is printed and there on celluloid is the image of innocence and simplicity Suresh has been seeking.

In the crassest of conventions, Shanti is to be propelled to stardom against her will. She is not an actress, she is *Devdas'*

Parvati, or as Suresh calls her simply 'Paro'. It is her total simplicity that attracts Suresh: she is a girl who knitted sweaters to support her way to matriculation. It is his passion for ideas and quest for simplicity that attracts Shanti. And it is their mutual desire to express the ideas encapsulated in *Devdas* that allegedly strikes a bargain between them.

From this point on, the making of a film version of *Devdas* is the calm centre of a frenzied world that is reiterating the themes of *Devdas*. Shanti becomes a puppet: the movie moguls would package her as a star in gorgeous sari and permed hair; to please Suresh she will spend a night with her head wrapped in a towel to undo the perm and remain Suresh's vision of Paro, the simple village woman who is the real India. The subtle play on public and private worlds that runs throughout *Kaagaz Ke Phool* paves the ground for the real tragedy of decency. Gossip published in a film magazine suggests a romance between Suresh and Shanti. His daughter's classmates taunt Pammi with 'the facts' in print and she runs away from school to confront Shanti. A different kind of eternal triangle, one created by a vain and fashionable world in conflict with enduring principles, means that all three central characters must suffer and lose. The celluloid image of *Devdas* is a great success, but public fame is the springboard to personal suffering. For the sake of Pammi, Shanti goes back to village India to teach, leaving only a knitted sweater to join the doll in Suresh's cupboard of memories. Suresh goes to court to reclaim his daughter and loses, and with his double loss begins a slide into self-destruction. Robbed of family and selfless love, his career evaporates, he degrades himself with drink and ends up a poor and destitute man given a job and shelter by his former driver. Meanwhile, public acclaim has brought Shanti back to the world of films to become a star and Pammi grows to womanhood and is to be married. On the eve of her wedding chance brings Pammi to the garage where her father now lives and works.

Suresh has rehabilitated himself in the midst of compassionate simplicity, but shame prevents him revealing his presence to the daughter who longs to make contact with her lost father. They are now part of different worlds, incommensurable worlds that cannot communicate.

To earn money to buy a wedding present for his daughter, Suresh asks a drinking companion to get him a job as a film extra. This is the man who directed *Devdas*, the friend announces, as prelude to a series of reflections on the fallen state of the once famous man. As an extra in an religious epic, Suresh must say the lines: "I am searching for peace (shanti), everlasting peace." As we see him bowed, ready to say his lines, the actress walks into shot: we see only her feet as she says, "Father, only those who can find no other path come here. Have you lost your way?" It is of course Shanti who asks the question to which Suresh can make no reply. Shanti alone recognises Suresh. He is thrown off the set and as a studio hand reclaims the shawl that envelops him, we see that he is wearing the sweater Shanti knitted, now torn and holed. Wordlessly he runs off and she pursues him, only to be caught in a crowd of adoring fans. And so we are back to the beginning of the film. Suresh wanders down from the lighting gantry to the floor of the studio and sits in the director's chair. When the crew arrive he is still sitting there and is recognised at last in death. The studio manager arrives and pushes his way through the mourning crowd and announces: 'Haven't you see a corpse before—get rid of it.' He marches off to the shout of 'Lights!', and on a dark screen as these points of light stare out THE END, the final credit appears, and we hear the closing theme:

Fly away O thirsty bee
You will find no honey in these raging torrents
Where paper flowers bloom
Visit not these gardens
Your naive desires have found a sandy grave

Your hopes are stranded on the shore
What the world gives with one hand
It wrests away with a hundred hands
This game has been played since time immemorial
I have seen people abandon me one by one
I have seen how deep friendship lies
I have seen people abandon me one by one
What have I gained from this world
I am left with nothing but tears...

From the first to the last frame, *Kaagaz Ke Phool* is a delicately crafted work of art. Its theme and juxtaposition is presented not just through the narrative, but also through songs. Despite their different moods and settings, all the songs—just as in *Mughal-e-Azam*—comment on the film's theme: even Shanti's seemingly innocuous song of numbers to her village schoolchildren culminates with the two lonely and alone numerals, one and nought, who found completeness as 10, being pulled apart by the envy and jealousy of the other numerals. Locating the central characters in the world of the film business is both their actual setting and a metaphor—indeed, what better metaphor for the selfishness of the world of modern manners? When Rocky discusses the 'tragedy of the year', a winning racehorse shot after breaking its leg, we know that it is not just the vacuous conversation of a playboy, but the wordplay of the only character in the film who seems to have everyone's number. When he asks what use is a three-legged race horse, Shanti, and everyone else, knows he is really speaking of Suresh. Rocky's incongruous hunting trip to the village is, after all, a considerate and compassionate effort to reunite Shanti and Suresh, and, as such, the film's episode of supreme irony.

Is *Kaagaz Ke Phool* just another reflection on the absurd cruelties of fate, before which decent people are impotent sufferers? The evidence would seem to be overwhelming. But ultimately even its most poignant lyrics, those that counterpoint the film and express its theme, are also ironic. The action of the film has shown the way of the world. The world of filmmaking in which the action takes place has conjured the shadow world, the dream of Devdas and Paro, a dream that is preoccupied with a yearning for a simple, noble India, for an innocence that has been lost and which endures in suffering. Love, in *Kaagaz Ke Phool*, is yearning of the lost and alone, love is also an understanding that looks beneath surface appearance, a joining and completeness. Is the unhappiness of *Kaagaz Ke Phool*, then, simply that Suresh and Shanti cannot, because of society's convention, be together?

The film admits of another interpretation: that neither of the central characters know how to cope with and channel selfless love into their lives as a positive force. Shanti's song sums up their predicament:

> You are no longer yourself
> I am no longer myself
> Our restless hearts rush to meet each other
> As though we have never been apart
> You lost your way
> I lost my way
> Though we had walked in step for such a little while
> Time has inflicted great cruelty on us
> You are no longer yourself
> I am no longer myself
> I can think of no place to go now
> I would walk away but no path is open to me
> What do I seek? The answer escapes me.
> I cannot stop my heart from weaving a tapestry of dreams...

Both respond to society's conventions with a decency the modern world clearly does not deserve, but as they gradually change places—Suresh sinking into the ignominy of the gutter while Shanti returns to the world of films, buys Suresh's old home and has a cupboard filled with old memories of unfinished pieces of knitting—it is they as people who have clearly failed to keep hold of something vital. It is not just fate, it is not just the selfishness of the world that separates and destroys them: it is their own inability to keep hold of the very best in themselves. Both Shanti and Suresh do the right thing; both base their actions on decency and propriety—values and sacrifice to which the selfish world around them remains oblivious. In doing what is right, however, they both diminish themselves and give themselves up to self-pity and bitterness and thus they destroy themselves. They can make nothing of the completeness of their mutual understanding, they cannot surrender themselves to the best in themselves and make a progression to a higher level of peace—the paper flowers of the world interpose themselves.

Kaagaz Ke Phool is a film of contradictions; it is at its most pithy when it appears to be most flippant and its strongest characters and villains are women. The web of fate is created by the unredeemable Veena, Suresh's estranged wife, who is no-one's puppet—especially not that of her bombastic father Sir B.B. Verma. She is a woman who glories in the power she possesses, the power of denial and depriving—she deprives Suresh of a home, companionship, love (if they ever did love each other) and his daughter. Her reward is that the Governor General will attend her daughter's wedding. The hand of fate is wielded by Pammi, Suresh's daughter—twice she interposes herself. First, as a child: claiming to understand everything, she confronts Shanti as the scheming woman who is keeping her parents apart, making it impossible for her to reunite them. But the child is as alone and abandoned as either of the central characters, and as active in creating her own abandonment. On the eve of her marriage to an empty-headed socialite she again runs away to search for her father and naturally demands that Shanti tell her his whereabouts. As child or woman Pammi seems incapable of any self-reflection on what she is asking or witnessing. The film's most pertinent comments on human relationships and especially women come from Rocky, the comic relief, who alone of all the characters acts with compassion for others.

Kaagaz Ke Phool contains all the hallmarks of a Guru Dutt film: a passionate revulsion of social inequalities, a hatred of materialism, a longing for the realisation of selfless love and an irrepressible idealism. The art form used both for criticism and examination of the theme in *Kaagaz ke Phool* is cinema; in *Pyaasa* (1957)—Thirsty—the same terrain is covered with poetry as the medium of discourse. The silent message of both films is essentially the same: art is an integral part of life, not just as a source of reflection, but also as a medium of positive social change.

Vijay (Guru Dutt), the protagonist of *Pyaasa*, is a poet in love with Meena, his former college classmate. But while Meena loves Vijay, she chooses to marry a rich man, Gosh. Because they are concerned with poverty, hunger and social inequalities, Vijay is unable to get his poems published, and finds it difficult to make a living. He is eventually thrown out of the family house by his selfish brothers who sell his poems as wrapping paper. One day, while wandering aimlessly, he hears a women reciting one of his poems. She turns out be Gulab, a prostitute, who had rescued his manuscripts and fallen in love both with the poet and his poems. Gulab devotes herself to Vijay who is so disgusted with the materialism and social inequalities he sees around him, and frustrated with Meena's actions, that he decides to commit suicide. But an act of kindness on his part, leads to the death of a beggar wearing his jacket. The world assumes that Vijay is dead. Gulab eventually persuades Gosh to publish his poems, which are an instant hit. Vijay's talent as a poet is realised and his death anniversary is celebrated with great fanfare. When it is discovered that Vijay is alive, all those who had deserted him—his brothers, Gosh, even Meena—suddenly gather around him and declare his greatness. But Vijay refuses to acknowledge his fame, declaring that he is not the same Vijay. He returns to Gulab and together they walk away 'far, far from this world'.

There are, in fact, four thirsty characters in *Pyaasa*. Vijay eventually rejects the materialistic world of Meena and accepts the world of Gulab which only increases his thirst for social justice and equality. When Vijay asks Meena to explain her betrayal, she says: 'Life is not just poetry and love, but also hunger.' She did not marry him because he could not support her financially. 'So you sacrificed your love for money,' replies Vijay. He is appalled not just by the fact that money is so important for Meena but also at the growing consumerism, and attendant dehumanisation, in India. When in a drunken stupor, he visits a prostitute who is dancing for her customers and hears her baby crying in the background, he not only feels pity for the woman but contempt for a society that has placed her there. He walks out of the den, falls in the street and sings what is undoubtedly the most powerful indictment of Indian society:

These streets, these action houses of happiness
These broken caravans of life
Where are the caretakers of dignity?
Where are those who take pride in India?

When he acquires fame, Vijay refuses to be seen as a commodity. 'I am not the Vijay that people are asking for,' he tells Meena when, following him desperately, she corners him in a library. 'Just what is your complaint?' Meena asks perplexed. Vijay replies:

I have no complaint. I have no complaint against any human being. My complaint is with that society which takes away humanity from human beings, which for small gains turns brother against brother, friends into enemies. My complaint is with a culture that worships the dead and treads the living under its feet, where crying two tears over other people's pain and sorrow are considered cowardice, where to meet someone in hiding is seen as a sign of weakness. I can never be happy in such a society.

We see Vijay walking away from Meena in a long shot where he is little more than a silhouette. A gust of wind forces books and paper from the library shelves to fly everywhere, as if to say that all this learning does little more than sustain the inequalities in the society that Vijay rejects.

Meena is materialism writ large. But all her wealth does not really satisfy her: her happiness is illusive. When Vijay meets her in the lift of Gosh's publishing empire, he imagines himself dancing cheek-to-cheek with her. The scene is deliberately unrealistic. For Vijay, she is just as unattainable as the happiness she seeks through materialism. The door of the lift closes to indicate that Meena is in fact in a prison: a prison of her own making. You have never understood, Vijay tells her, that one's own happiness is acquired only by maintaining the happiness of others. Meena has destroyed Vijay's happiness for money: she will always be thirsty.

Gulab is just as thirsty as Meena and Vijay. She longs for dignity as much as for Vijay's love. When she eludes a chasing policeman by accidentally running into his arms, and he saves her by saying that she is his wife, the expression of joy on her face signifies the momentary quenching of a thirst. He leaves her, but she follows him to a rooftop. Her emotions and desires are expressed by a passing street singer: 'Make me your own, hold me in your arms, satisfy my thirst...' Unlike Meena, she understands Vijay's quest and complaint: she is, after all, a victim of the society he despises. After Vijay's presumed death, she takes his poems to Meena, who typically asks: 'what do you want for these poems?' 'Price?' retorts Gulab. 'Can one place a price on beauty and questions of dignity?' The question is particularly ironic coming from a women who sells herself for money. In the final sequences of the film, Gulab hears someone calling out to her in her dreams. She wakes up and rushes out to the door of her house: it's Vijay. 'I have come to tell you that I am going away, far away.' 'You have come back only to tell me that?' 'I have come to take you with me.' Her face transforms with joy and the two lovers walk away together. But where is far? Towards death? A joint suicide pact? We know that Vijay has already tried suicide and it didn't work.

Perhaps the journey will take them far, as far as the location of the fourth silent character in the film: India, a new India.

The emergence of a new India depends, to a large extent, on the successful resolution of the old conflict between tradition and modernity. In Guru Dutt's films, modernity is always presented as rampant materialism that drowns the selfless love and innocence that is integral to tradition. There is no synthesis possible between the two: the one devours the other. But we are being presented with a very specific form of modernity: westernisation, Sir B.B.Verma and his family in *Kaagaz ke Phool* being the ultimate metaphor. When tradition and westernisation come together, helplessness and impotence is the only outcome. Dilip Kumar's *Gunga Jumna* (1961) explores the helplessness engendered by the clash of tradition and westernisation not from the viewpoint of a sophisticated film director or a radical poet, but from the perspective of a simple, uneducated peasant.

Gunga Jumna opens with a vision of village India and zooms in on one family, a widowed mother and her two sons, Gunga and Jumna, destined to follow the diverging paths of the holy rivers of the land. The mother is an icon of mother India, noble, devout, honest, sincere, but poor, hard-pressed and abused. The youngest son, Jumna, is the hope of the family, his hope is, as an early scene in his school suggests, iconographic and national—a good education to become a virtuous and hardworking citizen, a leader of tomorrow. The mother works as a maid for the second wife of the village landlord, who is 'a witch', proved by her being the only person in the village impervious to the integrity of the mother. In the brief exchanges between the wife and the mother are encapsulated the problems of the relationship between wealth and poverty: the one uncomplaining and enduring; the other high handed, abusive and oppressive. One such exchange takes place through a curtain when the mother brings water for the wife who has retired into her dressing room preparing to take her bath. Our point of vision is the mother; the device neatly underscores the remoteness of capricious power and its incomprehension of the reality it refuses to see.

The witch has a brother, whom we see being awoken from a drunken stupor by Gunga, the first unfortunate encounter of lives that are crossed and heavy with fatal implications. The brother is a well-to-do hanger-on, in need of money to indulge the pleasures of the flesh. While his sister bathes, he enters her room and takes her jewellery box. On the way to sell the glittering contents he throws the empty box onto a pile of dried cow dung where it is found by Gunga. The blame for the theft falls on the mother. The police search her home and find the empty box; she is imprisoned. The entire village, symbolised by the verbose, vacillating village clerk, knows this to be a gross injustice, the crime an impossibility for the suspected, alleged criminal, but there is no-one who can interfere with the workings of a remote and uninvolved system of 'justice'. That is, until the landlord himself arrives and agrees to post bail for the mother. She is released and goes home, but pierced by the shame and at last overwhelmed by this travesty in the name of justice she dies before the family altar.

This short opening prelude is quick and deft. The parameters of the film are set, its issues, characters and dramatic dynamic all drawn in rich vignettes, even the love interest is not neglected. We have seen Gunga with Dhanno, the stormy argumentative relationship, while Jumna has cast longing eyes upon Kamla, the landlord's daughter, the epitome of the quiet submissive ideal beauty. The love interest like the whole of this prelude is no thumbnail sketch. It is a representative icon so emblematic as to be instantly recognisable and therefore to suggest permanence and timelessness.

Time moves, visualised by the maturing of the harvest and the turning of the wheel of a bullock cart. Gunga and Jumna are now young men. Gunga, as irrepressible and lively as ever, is now working earnestly to provide for his brother's education, the dream of bettering the family's condition, of development, endures consuming the "sweat and blood" of the poor and is symbolised by the fountain pen Gunga has bought as a present for his brother, who is off to the city to finish his education. As his brother leaves, Gunga promises that Jumna can rely on his support as long as he lives: development will be driven by the efforts and aspirations of the poor who do not participate in the new horizons it opens. But for this idyll to succeed there must be peace, the peace of freedom from capricious oppression—and that is not the burden of Gunga Jumna's story.

By now the landlord has died, management of the estate is effectively in the hands of the witch's dissolute brother, who acts as if it were his own—the doubly rentier devoid of any sense of responsibility to a communal ethic. On his way to some debauched pleasure, the brother hears Dhanno singing in the woods and is stirred by thoughts of casual indulgence. He pursues her, intent on rape. Dhanno runs and screams, Gunga hears her cries, comes to her rescue and beats off the landlord. For this defiance there must be revenge. Gunga is framed for the crime of stealing grain, brought to court and sentenced to prison on bought, perjured testimony. In the face of a foreign system of 'justice' Gunga is rendered silent, submissive, shorn of his articulacy, made a mere pawn to be disposed of. No one speaks for him. This system of 'justice' is a tool of the wealthy, not a representation of the will of the people.

Gunga's concern is for his brother, whom he cannot support while in prison. He begs the village schoolteacher to provide for his brother and not to inform Jumna of his troubles, not to drag him back into the world of village oppression from which he is escaping. We see Jumna in a comfortable setting, working away among his books in his city lodgings. But this vision of golden opportunity cannot survive the abuses back home. The camera pans across Jumna's lodgings in the reverse direction to show them shorn of everything he has accumulated. Denied the support of his brother, he has sold everything; the camera ends its movement on Jumna picking up the last suitcase of his belongings, ready to leave his lodgings, but the landlord takes even that to compensate for unpaid rent. Destitute, Jumna takes to the streets. A crowd rushes by, chasing a thief, who drops a pearl necklace in the scramble to escape. At the police station we see the necklace returned to its owner. The inspector informs the flighty, urbanite owner that it is the honesty and integrity of Jumna that has secured the return of her property. Casual and careless, she offers Jumna a reward. When he replies that he has merely done his duty, she pockets the money and walks off. In the city, too, honesty is its own reward—it has no reciprocal financial obligations between rich and poor.

Gunga is released from prison to be met by Dhanno, the only person who has stood by him in his ordeal. He learns that Jumna has written to tell of his distress and ask why his brother has neglected him. Even the schoolteacher, who taught virtue and idealism, has let Gunga down. And still the landlord pursues Gunga, who takes to the hills with Dhanno, where they join up with a group of outlaws. Made an outcast, Gunga leads the bandits on raids against the landlord, though his life of crime is not particularly venal or successful. Back in the city, the inexorable forces of a blind and unresponsive system of justice are marshalling the final indignity. Jumna has been recruited into the police

117

force and is assigned to his native village of Haripur to root out the nest of bandits.

The train bringing Jumna back is set upon by the bandits, but they are fought off by the police contingent. Back in the hills Gunga learns that Dhanno is pregnant and that his brother has returned as police inspector and resolves to give up the life of an outcast. But he descends from the hills for one last defiance of the corrupt order. He bursts in on the arranged marriage of Kamla, taking place amongst a conspicuous display of wealth, insisting she will not be married against her will, without her consent. Gunga's 'crimes' are a different kind of justice, an insurgency against all forms of oppression. But they compel Jumna, whose virtue and aspiration has been co-opted by an alien institution of 'justice', to pursue his brother and usher in the final denouement.

Gunga surrenders himself to Jumna against the pleas of Dhanno, who has no faith in the system of 'justice' that will victimise her and their unborn child. The bandits descend on the jail where Gunga is held to liberate him and in the shoot-out Dhanno is fatally wounded. Gunga makes off to the hills with the dying Dhanno. Blundering through the smoke of her funeral pyre comes the landlord, whom Gunga shoots. In his torment he then goes to the village and sets light to the landlord's house. In the midst of the flames Jumna confronts his brother and the duty laid upon him by his office as police inspector. He has sought to use his position to bring charges against the landlord for suborning the perjury that put Gunga in prison, but the inflexibilities of this extraneous system are too little, too late and too inept to extricate the victims from the cycle of oppression that has enfolded them. Jumna is compelled to shoot his brother in the back as he seeks to escape. The dying Gunga makes his way back to his village home, the place we first saw him as a boy at the opening of the film. In this simple unchanging setting he seeks the only atonement and ultimate justice available to the poor—before the family altar he prays for forgiveness from the god and dies where his mother died, as his mother died, broken by the abuses of a corrupt system.

Gunga Jumna is an emblematic tragedy that wields its sophisticated analysis deftly. It presents itself as a powerful, emotional human drama. Its potency as social document is that its characters are what they are, they do not artificially, that is by clumsy crafting, represent and stand for the issues the film so directly and indirectly alludes to, they are rounded and real speaking in dialect, facing and enduring their specially dramatised story that is also so real as to be a commonplace of real life not celluloid tragedy.

It is a film of cleverly drawn heroes. Gunga (Dilip Kumar) is the most captivating hero: the spirit, independence and eventually the defiance of the traditional order, which, when pushed to the limit, becomes a resistance to the established order, its inequities, corruption and injustice. Jumna is the aspiring hero whose traditional virtues are co-opted and twisted into impossibly conflicting loyalties by the path laid out for progress, whose actual system is unable to resolve or immediately alleviate the competing claims for natural and legal redress of the world it has to deal with.

Most interestingly of all, it is a film of wonderfully drawn heroines. The mother is the heroic victim of the traditional order, with the resilience and power to endure everything except the perverse assault upon her dignity. Kamla too is an heroic victim, the woman suppressed and sacrificed by the oppressive system of traditional wealth, the woman with advantage made into a chattel to be exchanged against her will and without her consent. Both are, in their different ways, heroines, both in their different ways must be victims, because, in the final analysis, they are prepared to be submissive in the face of their oppression. The true, consummate heroine, matching Gunga in a profound sense, stretching from the superlatives of the performance by Vajentimalla to the barbs of their dialogue, is Dhanno. She is the possibility and potential of traditional woman as resistance and defiance, a theme as powerfully drawn as is Gunga's. Dhanno is independent, she earns her own living by her own "sweat and blood"; she is spirited, all her exchanges with Gunga and everyone else mark her out as self-possessed, capable, in charge of her own life; she is neither passive nor submissive, when events move she charts her own course standing by Gunga, advising him, counselling him and sharing his fate by her own choice and decision. Witty, articulate, intelligent, an independent motive for action, this is a heroine drawn directly from tradition—from the real meaning of traditional womanhood. Alongside Gunga, there is ever Dhanno, and between them there is a genuine, enduring and meaningful partnership. A man who not only wins but appreciates Dhanno could only have scorn for the Brahmin who seeks to prevent their marriage by arguing she is of a lower caste; such a man must make his last, most virulent, defiance of the established order by rescuing Kamla from her arranged marriage. The heroines' stories, the women's stories are not subplots and attendant detail, they are the story. Gunga has no doubts: he must defy the Brahmin and marry Dhanno. Jumna, throughout the film, acquiesces that the established order requires him to deny his love for Kamla and accept that their ideal match is impossible; not even his education and participation in development will resolve that dilemma. Gunga is triumphant in his tragedy because he sees clearly and acts to resist his oppression in partnership with Dhanno. Jumna survives tragically enmeshed in submission to incommensurable worlds, irreconcilable aspirations. Nowhere is the contrast more clearly made than in their relations with women and the nature of the heroines they cherish; the one heroine they share, their mother, and the two contrasting loves of their lives. Gunga Jumna is an indictment of corrupt tradition and complicit modernity; its challenge to the audience is explicit and lucid and centred on the question of

Curry on Scunthorpe!

Reporting on 'Eastern Eye'.

Zia, aged twelve, with his mother Hamida, sister Huma and brother Jamal.

Muqeet Mammu with two of his sons at my wedding.

Farid Mammu on his *charpoy*.

The 'Eastern Eye' interview with Dilip Kumar.

Hakim Abdul Raaiz Khan, *aka* Nana.

Nani Jaan.

Ehsan Danish in Mohammad Ali's house in Jeddah, with those appointed to look after him; he signed and dated the photograph (12 May 1978).

Waheed Mammu with my cousins Gudu and Puppu.

'Hazrat Baba Waheed Ahmad Khan Qalandari'.

Waheed Mammu's Mausoleum in Model Colony cemetery, Karachi.

The ceiling of the Mausoleum.

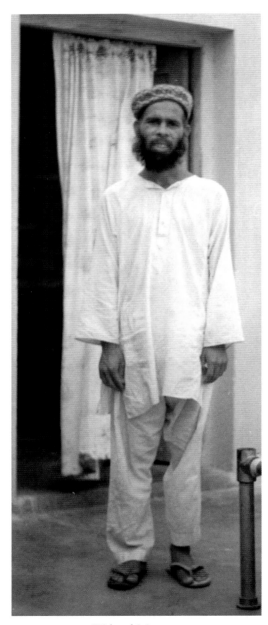

Waheed Mammu

women, for its human drama empowers women too as agents of cultural resistance and change.

There are a number of common threads running through *Gunga Jumna, Pyaasa, Kaagaz ke Phool, Devdas* and *Mughal-e-Azam*—the five main texts of my youth. All five texts are concerned, nay obsessed, in their individual way, with the idea of justice and the notion of unconditional love. All have a longing for and respect of the integrity of tradition. But none of them presents tradition as though it were an utopian goal—indeed, all five texts see traditional values as something perverted just as much by traditional society in history as commodified and framed by westernised modernity. It is not romanticised, traditional utopias that these films seek or promote; rather they argue for a tradition based on the integrity of its own authentic idealism. Indeed, in Guru Dutt's films there are only two options: suicide or return to traditional idealism. But even Guru Dutt's idealism is a rounded, all embracing idealism: it addresses women as well as men, it enables men to express feminine emotions and it seeks change in tradition as well as transformation in modernity. All five texts show women as strong characters. In *Mughal-e-Azam* the conflict is as much between Akbar and Salim as it is between Bahar and Anarkali: it is really the unwritten alliance between Akbar and Bahar that spells tragedy for Anarkali. In *Devdas*, Parvati is forced by social custom to acquiesce to her father's wishes but is strong enough to visit Devdas in the middle of the night—something no stereotypical traditional woman would ever do! And *Kaagaz ke Phool, Pyassa* and *Gunga Jumna* are replete with strong women making their own decisions, for good or bad. The aesthetic utilised in all five films is authentically Indian: taking its cue from classical tradition and folklore, representing India in all its diversity and multicultural layers, and seeking to influence, change and engage its audience purely on the basis of shared cultural assumptions.

As works of art, these films effortlessly combine different forms—poetry, music, dance—into an integrated whole through the energetic use of consummate visual imagination and superbly literate dramatic structures. The richness of these classical texts of my childhood is in their use of metaphor: the images on the screen are creative devices, dense and multi-layered constantly suggestive of connections and resonant with reference to wider cultural associations and ideas. Framing, composing, pacing, sound, rhythm, tonalities, poetry, language are all used to transform the image, to lift it beyond the simple needs of narrative, to describe it differently, thus making the visual image in itself another layer of complex metaphor. The filmmaker's metaphors are the essence of their reliance upon their audience. The audience cannot be passive, they are not taken for granted, and only they can complete the allusions, implications, suggestions and challenge of the metaphors—only they have the key to interpretation of the complex communication this cinema offers. This appeal to the audience is the trademark of a self-confident, domestic and domesticated metier of cultural production: a genuine Indian cinema, of India, for India. It is an Indian cinema made of the rapport, the shared culture and affinities of filmmakers and their audience. The metaphors of this medium then become a self-reflective vehicle for a whole society, a challenge to think, to discuss, to differ and to agree, to interpret variously and most of all to see its own condition rounded and contextualised in creative, suggestive and imaginative ways through the filmmakers' selection, juxtaposition and perspective. The metaphors define the aesthetic and ideological possibilities and become the yardstick for cinematic 'literacy' and intelligibility. A sophisticated film creates a sophisticated audience.

I grew up not just immersed in the metaphors of these texts, but thinking with them; they were part of my vocabulary, they were embedded in my imagination. My love of tradition, of

poetry and language; my distaste for social inequalities and concern for social justice; my devotion to unconditional, selfless
love; my quest to rescue traditional idealism from ossified traditional societies; my determination to act against the helplessness
and impotence generated by westernised modernity—can all be
traced back to the impact that Dilip Kumar and Guru Dutt had
on my imagination.

Modernity, in the form of his urban education and co-option
in an alienating system of middle-class justice, renders Jumna
totally passive. He is reduced to the expression of a single emotion: impotence. While Ganga is a complex character and capable, in his traditional simplicity, of a range of emotions and
actions, Jumna, the archtypical good urban-industrial man, is a
one-dimensional cripple. *Gunga Jamna* warns us about the
imminent arrival of a one-dimensional westernised, urban man.
It is the only film that also offers a prototype of possible solution: Ganga is cultural resistance writ large. He was to inspire me
both in my intellectual and practical endeavours.

IV

On my thirty-first birthday, I found myself at Rochdale General
Hospital. I was working on a story about the exploitation of
Asian doctors by the Health Service. I had discovered that the
Asian doctors were overwhelmingly employed in junior positions, their qualifications regarded as inferior and they were
mostly practising in areas generally shunned by their white col-
leagues (infectious diseases, for example, had large numbers of
Asian doctors). They were seldom promoted and were forced to
work incredibly long hours.

I was interviewing a doctor in his house near the hospital when
he was called on his beeper. The interview had just started and the
doctor asked if I could wait for his return. Without waiting for my
answer, he instructed his wife and children to entertain me, and

rushed off to the emergency. The children slipped a cassette in the video player and the entertainment began. It was *Sholay* (1975). I was appalled by what I saw. Here was the complex world of Indian culture filtered through a western lens and rendered totally incomprehensible. Here was the theme of Kurosawa's *Seven Samurai*, out of the regurgitation of *The Magnificent Seven*, spewed up as an Indian spaghetti western. Columbus insisted that Westward is the East; *Sholay* set out to prove it.

Sholay also represents a number of other departures from earlier films. In the film texts of my youth, and so many other films of that period, the religion of the characters is totally incidental: what matters is what they do and say. *Sholay* makes a conscious effort at representing Muslims, at portraying them, at enframing them. There are two Muslim characters in the film: one, Bhopali, is clearly a devious crook; the other, the blind Imam, is plainly a buffoon. In the cultural universe that is the India of *Sholay*, Muslims can exist only as criminals or impotent victims; no other role is conceivable for them. The women in *Sholay* are also ciphers. The sole function of Raddah, Jay's love interest, is to suffer her fate in silence. The only virtue of Basanti, Veeru's lover, is that she talks too much: what else is a woman good for? In *Gunga Jumna*, the rural simplicity of the villagers is presented as the bedrock of Indian society; in *Sholay*, their innocence is mocked. When Veeru threatens to commit suicide, in a staged attempt to persuade Basanti's mother to agree to their marriage, the following dialogue takes place between two villagers:

First villager: What is suicide?

Second villager: When the white people die they call it suicide.

First villager: Why do white people die?

First villager: What is good bye?

Second villager: When white people leave they say good bye.

First villager: Where do they go when they leave?

We are supposed to laugh at the exchange!

While the idealised notion of Ma is central to Amitabh Bachchan films, her own suffering and hardship are seldom examined in any detail. The Ma of these films is not 'Mother India' who endures and is adored, a potent symbol of womanhood as well as an individual who seeks the fulfilment of her own desires and aspirations. Here Ma becomes an empty vessel for an outpouring of cheap emotions; a vehicle for perpetual and misguided suffering; a hollow character whose existence is worked out through the desires and actions of the male characters: the son who must avenge the wrongs done to her and the husband or scoundrel who ruined her life. The motive of action, as in earlier Dilip Kumar and Guru Dutt films, ceases to be a function of women's choice. The other women in these films have no function except to be sought by men and dance and sing for their delectation. Their only aspiration is to be married, and, once married, to keep hold of their men. In *Faraar*, Raju's sister is only there to be raped and killed so that Raju can begin his quest for revenge. After killing his sister's rapist, he seeks refuge in the house of his former lover. She is only there to be dutiful—despite her love for Raju—to her husband, the police inspector out to catch Raju. In *Arjun*, Bima's educated sister is only there to prove that women cannot stand against a village tyrant: they can become easy victims of love and, even with education, they cannot stand up to male violence. In *Agneepath*, the sole function of Vijay's sister is to be kidnapped by the hero's enemies. Even when, as a young boy, Vijay is left to carry the body of his father, the sister is conspicuous by her absence. The women of contemporary Indian films are less liberated, less articulate, less persons than their forbears a generation ago. The question of women has been resolved in today's films by reinforcing the most bizarre aberrations of rigid traditionalism. In vapid films vapid women walk backwards into a cultural realm of oblivion; as social personalities they have become necessary set dressing and sources of temporary musical diversion. They are the belle dames to be rescued, not ingredients of the narrative.

While mothers are idealised icons, and sisters are ciphers, fathers are the root of all evil. They seem to have developed the habit of abandoning the mother without ever making an honest woman of her. In *Trishul*, R K Gupta impregnates Shanti, the hero's mother, and then opts for a wealthy suiter. In *Namak Haram*, Vijay's industrialist father not only ruthlessly exploits the workers—'the English have left us a great legacy', he tells Vijay, 'divide and rule: divide them on ethnic grounds, keep the workers divided'—he is also the source of division between Vijay and his ever-so-loyal friend, Chander. In *Suhaag*, the hero's mother is not only called Durga, she is actually presented as a goddess of motherhood. Her husband, the gangster Vikram—played by Amjad Khan—refuses to acknowledge her as his wife after she gives birth to twins. The twins are separated: Amrit, Amitabh Bachchan, is bought by a dissolute criminal and grows up to a life of crime; Kishen, the inevitable Shashi Kapoor, is brought up by the mother and becomes a police inspector. Not only are they unaware they are brothers, they have no idea the villain they jointly pursue is their father. When Kishan is blinded by Vikram, Amit assumes his role as a police inspector to continue the quest. Driven to desperate measures as the pursuit closes in, Vikram takes refuge in the home of the women he ruined. This reunion has only one possibility, preposterously hurried into being: a woman stands by her man, no matter what he has done, what he has become and will defend him to the very last. But even such female selflessness is insufficient to redeem an evil father: it is only sons that move him. In the final fight scene, Vikram learns the identity of his two sons, and the brothers discover the real meaning of the bond that has drawn them together and set them against the evil that shaped their lives. Brothers must stand together; fathers must get their come-uppance; the existence of sons instantly changes Daddy and prompts his expiation of his numerous wrongs. Elsewhere, Daddy may take the bullet intended for his son. In *Suhaag* he becomes the donor; in an organ transplant of superb ingenuity, he gives his eyes to the son he blinded! In prison uniform, with two white patches where once his eyes were, he takes leave of his sons a better man.

Plumbing the range of human relationships in contemporary Indian films has become immersion in complication with no hint of complexity and with the addition of emotional lobotomy. The family is a mystic entity, a primal bond that occasions the working of fate and whose links endure magically to outwit the worst that fate can throw at individuals. The family becomes a convention that is neither explored nor scrutinised but only serves to impel preposterous plot lines. The rationale of the family is only to be, and what it is is a hackneyed version of the most prosaic kind of conventional dictum. Whereas in *Gunga Jumna*, the tragedy of the brothers is moving because of the reality of the life they have shared and what they have given, received and invested in each other, in the genre of Amitabh Bachchan the fellowship between individuals is really explained by the fact that unbeknownst to them they are brothers. It isn't sufficient for them to be drawn together as human beings with shared experiences; their friendship arises from the fact they are really brothers. Trite emotions follow the inevitable revelations of family connection, characters immediately fall into line with what convention deems such family ties should contain and imply. But the family has no real existence.

The only thing that really exists in the Amitabh Bachchan genre, the films of late seventies and eighties, is the emotionless, angry young man out for revenge. Revenge is equated with justice, and to this end any means can be justified. The formula for the plot is summed up in the pre-credit opening of *Faraar*. In an attempt to save her honour, a young girl kills herself by jumping from a boat. Despite his efforts, her brother, Raju, a painter, cannot prove the guilt of the assailant, who is acquitted by the courts. Raju stands in front of his painting of his sister and swears: I promise you Mita, I will avenge your blood. I will avenge, Mita. I want my right. I want justice. Justice.

And how is this justice to be sought? In Suhaag, Amit provides the standard answer. When Amit agrees to become the eyes of the blinded Inspector Kishen, Kishen asks him to ensure that in pursing the villain he stays within the law. Amit replies: I do not know what is and what is not against the law. I know only this: I cannot rest until I bring darkness in the life of the man who took the light of your eyes.

When the moment of revenge finally arrives, it has to be played out with stylised brutality. Why? In Trishoul, Vijay gives the conventional answer:

I am taking account of my mother's tears.
Every tear becomes a kick in the face!

The kick is not just a flailing leg but also a sound blast. The stylised fight sequences in the Amitabh Bachchan genre of films are just as much a product of formula as the narratives themselves. There is the jump from the rooftop. The mid-air, gravity defying somersault. The punch that sounds like an explosion. The *tish-tish* karate chop. Since violence is the *raison d'être* of the narrative of so many of these films, the fights appear as natural phenomenon. The song and dance routines, however, are totally postmodern disjunctions.

In the classical films of Dilip Kumar and Guru Dutt, song and dance were not added extras. They were part of the poetry of the narrative. When, in *Mughal-e-Azam*, Anarkali sings of her plight in prison, she articulates her emotions in verse and sums up the narrative to that point. Furthermore, we have no problem in believing that it is Anarkali who is singing: after all, she is a poet, and, as a courtesan, she sings for a living. And this is exactly what Bhadur Shah Zafar, the last Mughal emporer, did: he wrote and sang poetry in the Rangoon prison to which he was exiled by the British. In Pyaasa, the poet-hero, Vijay, sings his own poems, which also elaborate the humanist and socialist message of the film. When Gunga or Dhanno sings in Gunga Jumna, they sing in the village dialect in which they speak. In *Kaagaz ke Phool*, the film director hero, Suresh, does not sing at all—it would be against his character—instead, we have the elaboration of his emotional state through the songs on the soundtrack. Again, Dev Das does not sing: he is clearly too emotionally distraught to do anything so daft. Another Dilip Kumar classic, Jogan, contains numerous songs. But they are all *bhajans* (Hindu devotional songs), sung by the heroine who is a mystic: singing *bhajans* in temples is her vocation. Even the playback voices were matched to the actor and character. It was attention to such detail that made the total package work as art.

In these classical films, songs have a narrative reason. The songs stretch the genre to make the final product, the film, a form of total communication, a work of art. It is the songs which often elaborate the resonance and implications of the emotional, intellectual and social import of the action. The juxtaposition, counterpoint and seamless integration of songs that are superb poetry is the distinctive mark of a cinema that could only be Indian, of the formation and vibrancy of a genre of authentic cultural expression. No cinema in the world has merged such discrete spheres of art, probably no other cinema could. But the effectiveness of this art form depends on the sensitivity, the artistic logic of the fusion; to work, it can never stretch the audience's sense of logic and appropriateness too far. If they sing, and when they sing, the characters must be in character, just as the poetry must capture the character, mood and essence of the drama we are engaged in. Hardly surprising, then, that the songs

129

themselves are pure poetry at its most effective: they were written by *bona fide* Urdu poets. Indeed, almost all the great Indian Urdu poets of recent times have written songs for films. Josh Malihabadi, Arzoo Lucknavi, and later: Majaz, Kaifi Azmi, Khumar Barabankvi, Akhtarul Iman, Sahir Ludhianvi, Shakeel Badauni and Hasrat Jaipuri. Khaifi Azmi not only wrote the lyrics of *Kaagaz ke Phool*, but was also responsible for the film of the classical love story, *Heer Ranja*, which is written entirely in rhyming couplets. Sahir Ludhianvi wrote the lyrics for *Pyaasa* and published an anthology of his film poems. Shakeel Badayuni wrote the lyrics for both *Mughal-e-Azam* and *Gunga Jumna*, as well as published numerous anthologies of his poems.

In the films of Amitabh Buchchan and those who followed him, song and dance routines are just that, songs and dances. They owe their origins not to a distinctive art form, nor do they continue the tradition of another distinctively Indian art form, the cinema. They are derivative ditties of international pop music, slightly tempered to Indian tastes. They decorate in the most trivial way stories whose complicated, overlong working out they complicate further by abrupt interruption. They have little or no connection with the narratives, they take no account of characterisation, and, above all, their lyrics are totally meaningless. There is something absurd afoot when, in *Namak Halal*, a supposedly simple, semi-literate villager walks into a five-star hotel and begins to sing a disco number, or a gangster—a standard Amitabh Buchchan character—in *Pukar* suddenly busts into song and dance. It is giving the product specification of the production line of contemporary Indian cinema too much credit to say their use of song and dance was postmodern (before the concept was ever invented) and that it outclasses theatre of the absurd (without ever seeking to know the genre even exists)—yet these are the categories they inevitably bring to mind. The increasingly absurd disjunctions of the increasingly elaborate song and dance sequences is the death knell of the cinema as drama and fits it to be only minimalist entertainment of the lowest common denominator.

In earlier films, poems fitting the narratives were written first and a tune based on the lyrics was developed later. In the Amitabh Buchchan genre, the process is reversed. Tunes based on western pop music are produced first and then meaningless words are added to them later. For example, a song from the highly successful *Trishul*:

Gaputchi, Gaputhci Gum Gum
Kishi, Kishi, Cum Cum
I wish we may stay together forever!

The title song of *Namak Halal* actually tries to wrench some meaning from the absurd situation in which it is sung:

The elders say: stand on your feet
And the time will be with you
Walk with the wind
And All songs will be yours.

The opening song of *Geraftaar*—in which, 'above all', Amitabh Bachchan appears 'in a very special role' (namely a police inspector who beats everyone to pulp)—is sung in a bizarre postmodern setting with the side hero doing stunts for a film:

I will open the lock of fate
I will become an actor with a name
I need your prayers!

More recent songs do not even bother to use words. A recent hit disco number goes something like this:

1,2,3,4,5,6,7,
8,9,10,11,12,13!

Needless to say, the song has absolutely no connection with the narrative of the film. It need not be so. Even numbers can make a song poignant, as *Kaagaz Ke Phool* so elegantly proved.

When Shanti returns to her village and becomes a schoolteacher, she enchants her class by turning a lesson on numbers into song, a familiar and, in dramatic terms, an acceptable device. This innocent little song becomes a reflection on the central tragedy of the film; it adds to the development of the narrative by demonstrating that even in useful exile Shanti has found no peace and is haunted by her unhappiness.

This kind of 'poetry and refinement', laments the film musician Naushad, who wrote the music for *Mughal-e-Azam* and *Gunga Jumna*, 'has gone out of the window'. Songs are written in banal prose: 'Sit up, sit down, stand up, its raining; something happened, something didn't. This is not poetry.' Fitting lyrics to imported tunes is like saying 'a coffin is ready, bring a corpse that fits its size'. Naushad continues: 'The films that we make today are Indian only in name. We do not find India in them. In them all the things are foreign to Indian culture... The music, the story, the dress are all foreign. Indian-ness is totally absent... where we stand today is only a place of despair and sadness'.

V

On my thirty-second birthday, I met Dilip Kumar—and found happiness again!

A few weeks earlier, I had met Amitabh Bachchan. He had agreed to appear on 'Eastern Eye' while in London for a concert tour. He arrived at the studio with a collection of his bodyguards and throughout his brief stay at the television studio he remained aloof, talked little and smiled even less. He was dressed the way he always dresses in all of his films: no matter what film he is in, what character he portrays, he always ends up wearing the same set of sweaters, leather jackets and white suits. On this occasion he was in his white uniform. Most of the programme was handed over to him. He admired the 1,500 portraits of him sent by

'Eastern Eye' viewers and talked largely about where he had been, his accident and his role as the Angry Young Man. 'I like these roles,' he said, 'there is something of me in them.' And: 'In the hearts and minds of the youth of India, there is a hidden anger—in these roles, the way they are written, the way they are performed, they have found a release.' He spent most of the interview answering banal questions from viewers about his height, weight, children, dogs, and the most embarrassing situations he had experienced.

Amitabh Bachchan, it became clear to me, may be a star, but he was not an actor. He is not the kind of actor who reflects on the genre he has created, or the phenomena that is Amitabh Bachchan. In interview after interview over the course of his meteoric career, he has pointedly declined to engage in any discussion or analysis of his films, their impact or effect. The profession of the actor is to be a vehicle; there is no law that states all actors must be self-reflective. But there is something ominous about the power of a popular culture that has become so singularly personified, and where that singular personification so exactly mirrors the lack of self-consciousness of the product. In the studios of Eastern Eye, he appeared exactly as he appears in all of his film: Amitabh Buchchan, a personality, aloof and emotionless, strangely cold and absent. In life, as in his film, he runs the whole gamut of his emotions from A(mitabh) to B(achchan), as Dorothy Parker would undoubtedly have said.

I knew that on film Dilip Kumar could summon up an infinite reservoir of emotions: he could grab and hold one's attention and feelings and release them at will; his presence forced one to look and listen not just with attention and admiration, but also with certain awe and reverence. But what was the celluloid hero of my childhood like in real life? Would he be cold and distant, withdrawn and reserved, conscious of his star status, like Amitabh? Would he be like *Devdas*: introverted, inarticulate, incoherent?

Would he be like the hero of *Aan*: debonair, dashing, demanding? I knew from my initial research that he was a literary man—indeed, when he first began acting in films in 1944, he was the secretary of the literary society of his college. I also knew that he had a traumatic childhood. He grew up in a village not too far from the Khyber Pass, where he had witnessed a great deal of violence, and was once stranded, at the age of six, near Peshawar City Square with three dead bodies. Were the childhood scars still visible in his personality? I feared—nay, expected—my film hero to have feet of clay in real life!

When I went to interview him for 'Eastern Eye', I found him wandering in the lobby of the hotel. He was joking with the waiters and then became involved in a deep conversation with a doorman. It was an animated conversation; he was repeating the sentences of the doorman with certain pleasure, savouring each word individually. The image of Gunga from *Gunga Jumna* came to my mind: I detected the same innocence and verve. I waited for him to finish. After a while, I began to get annoyed at the fact that he kept both myself and the crew waiting while he finished his conversation with the doorman. Eventually he came over, greeted me, read my thoughts and put his hands around my shoulders: 'I too was impatient when I was your age,' he said. And then explained that the doorman spoke a unique Indian dialect. 'You know all these provincial languages have got a beautiful flavour of their own and they reflect nativity. I have a great weakness for these languages including Marathi and Punjabi.' He had a Behari gardener, he said. 'He always used to rebuke me, always affectionately; he and his wife wouldn't speak anything else but their village dialect. Wouldn't it be nice to do a film in this dialect, I thought.' He did. It was *Gunga Jumna*, in which he not only starred, but also wrote and produced, as well as directing it under the pseudonym of Natin Bose.

Great actors are chameleons, assuming their characters as their very self. Extraordinary actors are something else again—something not even the miscellany of mythic creatures yet has a name for. That is something of the impression one gets from meeting Dilip Kumar. An encounter with him is a double bonus: two amazing, rounded and culturally refined personalities in one individual. There is Dilip Kumar the actor, who after a string of emotionally wrought roles in such films as *Devdas, Mughal-e-Azam* and *Jogan*, found himself under emotional strain. 'You tend to become more and more grim, your responses become a little heavy and you keep on doing grim tragedies... People cave in under the influence of these assumed personalities, not only of the work they do on the screen but the hell of stardom.'

What kept him together was his real self: Yusuf Khan. When Dilip Kumar finished a day's shooting he returned home to his true identity as Yusuf Khan:

> when you come back home and you lie down on the bed and the room is there and everything is still. You feel all of this. There is an element of unreality about cinema because all of a sudden when the lights are on, the whole story vanishes. The palace has gone and so has the orchard or the rivers, the landscapes, the hardship and the resplendent moments of it. Likewise, an actor when he comes back he has to come back to himself—back to the fan and the cold air-conditioned room with the drone of the air-conditioning and you have got to go to sleep. You have to wipe everything off the mind, you've got to clean the slate, and face another day...I think the individual personal self is more important because that's what you live with. When working one has to have a no nonsense approach about the vital issue of your work because there is the work which has to be addressed—you have to address yourself to it and there is the personal personality which is the basic equipment with which you are playing so it should remain in good condition. One should not lose one's own sense of tranquillity.

But how does one ensure 'personal tranquillity'—a sense of ease with one's Self? The standard formula is to withdraw from society, to keep your private life private, to surround yourself by bodyguards and PR people who keep you away not just from admiring fans but also from society at large. But for Yusuf Khan, serenity comes not from withdrawing oneself from the public but by being involved: 'You cannot be immune to your surroundings.' Personal health and sanity is a function of your 'awareness of the conditions around you'. This is why 'you have to get involved in social and civic phenomena of society around you because no actor, for that matter no citizen, can develop in a vacuum of his own. An actor has to participate in the lives of the people and the problems of the people who give him his currency.'

Hence, Yusuf Khan became one of the most popular Mayors of Bombay.

I know nothing of Bombay. But the India of my childhood was a land of cultural pluralism where what mattered was not one's personal creed, but how one related to this rich diversity, what one contributed towards the evolution of a multicultural, multi-ethnic, multilingual identities, and how one promoted harmony and a sense of peace amongst different groups. Of course, there were always disputes and conflicts. The source of these conflicts, however, was never ethnic or religious, but, as in *Gunga Jumna*, a feudal heritage, or, as in *Mughal-e-Azam*, different set of principles, or, as in *Pyaasa* and so many other films, tradition and modernity. However, India, my India, was always above the banalities of religious chauvinism and ethnic arrogance. What I heard in this interview was the voice of the India of my childhood—the India that I always kept in my mind's eye:

> The scene in India is very splendid. There are Hindus, there are Muslims, there are Christians, there are Sikhs, there are Buddhists, there are Parsees all living there. Then there are varied provincial cultures which are so individualistic and so distinct. It's like the colours of a rainbow. That's the essence of Indian culture. So one has got to be aware; and one has also to be aware of the shortcomings

and own up to these shortcomings—not gloss over them. I think the responsibility of an actor in the present day society is to cultivate a sense of awareness and try to stimulate himself and try to imbibe all that's positive in these various cultures, various schools of thought.

I asked Dilip Kumar about the plight of Muslims in India. His face changed: there was agony there; there was frustration; there was some confusion too. I remembered a haunting scene from *Andaz*: the hero learns that the woman he loves has only been playing with him; this is the 'modern way', she says; she is actually going to marry someone else. The camera moves slowly and settles on Dilip Kumar's face: there, in that agonising hold that seems to last forever, the entire contradiction of tradition and modernity, the misery of betrayal and the confusion of new secular values, is worked out on his face. Yusuf Khan composes himself:

It's necessary for the Muslim community to live, live in good conditions, develop good mental health, and be economically viable with
the rest of the society, because if they are left from the mainstream
of growth then they are bound to become a menace to society and
that's why I am involved with Muslim education, economic development, Muslim community's life, the same way as I am involved with
the institutions of the Sikhs or with the Christians.

The extent of his involvement became quite evident during the 1993 Hindu-Muslim riots in Bombay. He mobilised the film community to help the Hindu and Muslim riot victims, he led missions inside the slums of Bombay to rescue besieged Muslims, who would otherwise have surely been butchered, and he transformed his house into a refuge for the victims of riots.

The rise of Hindu fundamentalism, the persecution of Muslims, the marginalisation of other Indian minorities, the fissures and fragmentations in the Indian personality, the banish-ment of art and poetry, and the consequent decline of the Indian cinema, are all products of the evaporation of Indian culture, that culture which is portrayed so elegantly, so forcefully, so honestly, in the early films of Dilip Kumar and Guru Dutt. The Indian cinema is not just a product of, but also one of the main reasons for, the fading of Indian culture. Cultural concerns, said Dilip Kumar, have been replaced in the Indian films by action, 'a lot of ingenious ways of smuggling narcotics and killing of people', and an 'obsession with Western culture'. 'You can import textile machines, you can import know how of various sorts, but you can't import culture, you can't import literature. That has to grow from the grass roots, from the soil itself.' When Indian cinema ceases to be Indian, it is not just the movies that are 'increasingly impoverished'. The 'masses in India have a limited range of diversions, they don't have football and soccer and rugby or other recreational sports like fishing, swimming, hiking, jogging: they either work or they go to the cinema', and increasingly take their values from what they see on the screen. An improvised cinema has produced an improvised Indian society.

In *Shakti*, Dilip Kumar and Amitabh Bachchan are brought together. Dilip Kumar plays Ashuni Kumar, a highly principled police inspector who, even when his only son, Vijay, is kidnapped by gangsters, refuses to compromise. The son, as usual, grows up to be the archetype—angry, emotionless, individualistic—Amitabh Bachchan. He utters the standard Amitabh lines: 'I am afraid only of myself,' he tells Ruma, his future wife, after he rescues her from thugs; when he is ready to go and beat the main villain to pulp (Om Puri yet again), he declares: 'the justice I seek needs neither a witness nor any evidence, it needs neither a court nor any law... I make my own law'; and again, returning from a mission of vengeance: 'I have come in this world alone, I will live alone, I will die alone. Whatever I will have to do, I will do it alone.' The acting and the expression of emotions is left to Dilip Kumar, whose power and presence on the screen truly dwarfs Buchchan. Presciently, the film script utters my own conclusion on these two stars of the two eras of Indian cinema. The differ-

138

ence is amiably expressed when Ashni Kumar's wife, Shital compares the character of father and son. She tells Vijay: 'Even if you
die ten times and are reborn ten times, you will not be able to
have his qualities.'

VI

On my thirty-eighth birthday, the Asian community of Britain
acquired a new voice: the 24-hour Sunrise Radio. For the first
time in Britain, Sunrise provided a platform, a meeting place in
the air, where different segments of the Asian community could
discuss, in their own local languages and dialects, issues of common interest and comment on each other's perceptions. Within
months, Sunrise acquired a huge following for its diet of film
songs, chat, constant stream of congratulatory birthday and
anniversary messages and news, sandwiched between a remark-
able amalgam of gaudy advertisements, including an endless
stream of plugs for the station itself: 'Do you want to make more
money? Increase your sales? Then advertise on Sunrise Radio.'
   A daily dose of Sunrise radio for a couple of weeks is enough
to confirm the fact that the British Asian community is quite
ignorant of its constituent parts. The Hindus have little knowledge of the Muslims; the Muslims know next to nothing about
the Hindus. The ignorance separating the two communities
begins with the 'morning worship'. We have *bhajans*—Hindu
devotional songs—for the Hindus; and *qawwalis*, heretical-cum-
devotional songs for the Muslims. Only an amoeba would assume
that the two are the same and play a similar function for the two
communities. The presenters have problems in recognising the
diversity of the Asian community. The Hindu presenters can't
get themselves to say *Slamu 'alaykum*, or peace be upon you, the
traditional Muslim greeting; the Muslim presenters just about
manage a half-hearted '*Namaskar*'. Both varieties, then, continue

to address their audience as though they were a large, amorphous mass with a monolithic religious identity.

During my childhood, the two communities came regularly together in the local cinema where they had an opportunity to socialise as well as to learn from each other. Nowadays, British Hindus and Muslims have no real physical contact with each other; except perhaps in schools or their workplaces where they are deracinated by the nature of the British conventions they have to deal with, leaving them no space to work with or work out the attendant issues of the diversity of their Asian identity. The perceptions of the two communities about each other are largely drawn from the Indian cinema which, as a melange of undigested and indigestible ingredients, itself harbours echoes of so many Western prejudices that fragment and misrepresent Asians to each other and themselves. The most popular programmes on Sunrise radio are the phone-ins, and it is here that the fragmentation of the Asian community, and what the modern Indian films have etched on its psyche, becomes most evident. At best, the Hindu callers to various phone-in programmes of Sunrise, such as 'Forum' and 'J K Show', seem to see Muslims as some sort of symbolic 'Other' of the Subcontinent; one needs to give them a nod or two in recognition, but nothing more is needed. The Sunrise voices of the Hindu community relate to Muslims just as the Hindu hero of *Deewar*, Viajy/Amitabh, relates to the presence of Islam in India: he keeps the numerological representation of Bismillah (In the name of God), 786, as a lucky charm round his neck, touching, playing with it now and again, to confirm its existence! Or, as in *Zanjeer*, where the hero's sidekick is a Muslim, the entire Muslim community is seen as 'also ran': making an effort, but not really important or all that trustworthy, unlikely to get anywhere; in the end, it is the Hindu hero who is going to save the day. These, of course, are the better perceptions: quite often the Muslims are cast in terms of the brainless, fanatical, blind 'Imam Shahib' of *Sholay*: ciphers with tendencies to emotional outbursts. The Muslims, on the other hand, always perceive the Hindus as dominant and dominating, when not conspiring, then simply out to get even for historic injustices, like Amitabh Bachchan in so many of his films!

This has been the perpetual pattern of exchange among Hindus and Muslims on Sunrise. A discussion on Kashmir, for example, has numerous Hindu callers insisting that Pakistan is a terrorist state and the uprising in Kashmir can be blamed solely on the violence that Muslims are so prone to. Two communities talked totally past each other in a discussion on the sacking of the Babri mosque in Ayodhya. Suddenly all of India became hell-bent on avenging the historic injustices done by Muslims; Muslim callers declared that Hindus would understand nothing less than the full might of 'jihad'. Even less politically sensitive subjects like birth control draw blood: Hindu callers described Muslims as antiquated and intrinsically anti-birth control; the Muslims perceived that Hindus were bent on secularising and demeaning their religion.

Most of the young male voices one hears on Sunrise, particularly during the late night phone-ins, resemble that of a hero who has rejected traditional morality and who, in his solitary loneliness, is standing up to the rest of the Asian world. I am what I am; if you don't like what I am, stuff you. I know how to fight back and will be happy to oblige. It's Vijay versus Thakur—and we know who always comes out on top. Even such Sunrise programmes as *Mahfil* and *Sada Bahr*, literary phone-ins which serve as a back-handed compliment to Urdu poetry, are not free from accusatory shouting bouts. One regular Hindu patron of *Mahfil* upsets another regular by making less than complimentary comments about the Prophet Muhammad's attitude to poetry—a great deal of abuse and mudslinging follows. Tempers fray, passions let fly, but the on air reconciliation is also as prompt and as phony as in the films. The offended and offending parties make up almost instantly and the air reverberates with a forgiveness that has no roots in genuine rapprochement of the minds. It is a sensibility for civility that can make do without any sense or sensitivity to actual issues that provoked the argument in the first place.

As in cinema, so in real life women serve a different function. For a large segment of traditional Asian women, Sunrise appears to be the only connection they have with the outside world. Women listeners phoning in to programmes like *Rang-e-Hinna* tend to talk about their own lives and problems. Each life thus narrated over the air echoes the basic themes of modern Indian cinema: the rants against the evil father/husband (who, in the end, is always supported); the tragic break-up of families due to 'misunderstanding' or tradition or on account of certain (imagined?) nefarious doings on the part of a 'villain' (mother-in-law, the other woman); the obsessive Ma who refuses to let go of her daughter/son; and, finally, the request for that song from that film which articulates it all with the meaninglessness of its lyrics. 'My mother is too possessive; she won't give me my freedom'; 'My mother is forcing me to marry a boy I haven't met and don't know'; 'My mother-in-law has become a wall between me and my husband. She is tearing us apart'; 'My daughter doesn't respect me. She is refusing to marry my nephew'; 'My husband has taken to drinking. He is ignoring me and my children'; 'We are celebrating our wedding anniversary can you play that song from ...'. Each life, it appears to me, an occasional eavesdropper on these chat-cum-family melodramas, is an Indian film *par excellence*!

Sunrise radio serves as both a personification and an outlet for the internal anxieties that the Asian community feels at the loss of its sense of belonging. It echoes both the fragmentation of British Asians as well as their frustrations at not being able to relate to each other. Its language, perceptions, feuds, frivolities, gestures, as well as the personal narratives that are its common fare, appear to come straight out of the celluloid. Both the station itself and its patrons exist and act within the well established formulas of contemporary Indian films.

The formulaic nature of Hindi films has been a frequent cause for concern among many eminent Indian critics. In *Our Films, Their Films*, Satyajit Ray wraps minimal analysis in a bored reflection on a genre he mercifully transcended. The Indian film, with its standardised song and dance routines, romance, tears, guffaws, fights, chases and melodrama, he writes, is 'directed mainly towards tapping latent responses in the audience'. It does 'not call for the evolution of new symbols, but the pinpointing of familiar fragments of visible reality and endowing them with a particular meaning in a particular context'. The Indian film critic Satish Bahadur, on the other hand, sees the formula only in terms of product specification:

> Largely a mixture of songs, dances, fights, suspense, and comedy, with hardly any kind of specialization. This omnivorous appeal is its greatest single feature. It goes from one extreme to another to entertain and appease its large composite audience; not wishing to give offence to any section, it is torn between a conservative pose and a modernist stance—it can neither turn its back on its patrons who belong to the more traditional ethos, nor put off the more modern who welcome change.

Both seem to miss the essential point. Commercial, pedestrian and contrived it may all be, yet the formulaic movie is a new kind of Indian mythology, rooted inescapably in the more suffocating strands of traditionalism that have survived in India, and which, aided and abated by the Indian cinema, became entrenched amongst the British Asians. Indeed, one might go so far as to say it is the epitome of stultified and ossified traditionalism made afresh. For it is conformity with the brain extracted, it is convention without reason, minus the humanity, the emotional range and resonance of a living organism. It is mythology as abstract amoeba. The formula is the metaphysics of the social context in which these films exist.

Whereas in the heyday of classic Dilip Kumar and Guru Dutt cinema, Indian films not securely placed in time were replete with references to contemporary issues, their themes anchored them and gave them cultural resonance. The new era of Indian filmmaking has warped time and space. The overly convoluted storylines, especially in the films of Amitabh Bachchan, describe a loop, a cyclical peregrination of fate that has reduced cultural reference to a parody of a set of principles. The wheel of life, the cyclical ages of time become circular tales of a wrong committed and the centrifugal forces that whirl the principal participants into a final denouement where that wrong is revenged. The wider world is a pastiche on which these dramas are hinged but which impinges on them hardly at all. Deeply embedded in each pre-posterous storyline is a conventional traditional symbolism that reverberates with stage dressing nuances of Hindu religious ideas rendered to their lowest common denominator. The cycle never changes, just as it is always Holi—the festival of colour—in Hindi movies.

Just as deeply embedded in the metaphysic is the coded essence of modernity. The modern era of Indian filmmaking is redolent of modernity, full of the instrumentalism of power, embodying the traits of the modern world so completely into its one dimensional characters that it has nothing to say about modern times. Its hero, the contemporary cinematographic hero, is an agent of personalised getting even, the wish fulfilment icon in a world of alienated ideas and ideals. This hero, whatever his origin, whatever his trajectory in endless pot-boiling stories is equivocal, standing on the fringes of legality, a worldly wise, hustling, likeable rogue—whose great charm is that he can make the laws of the street work to his individual ends. With vaults and leaps, and a smart kick in the face, he can break the cycle of wrong in each story. But his adversary is a single character, a person as personless as the hero himself, so the victory remains personal, an individual settling of scores. The cycle goes on; only the individuals caught up in the wheel change. Modernity rules (OK) and traditionalism endures the turning of the ages, and neither has any self-reflection or comment on the other—what is there to say about the forces that define the ambit of existence? The only choice for the individual is to make their way as best as they can, to endure the bludgeoning of fate by all the chicanery they can muster. It represents the very worst of a cynical opinion of the most distorted view of both traditional morality and modern amorality. That is the potency of this new symbolism of the emergent metaphysics of contemporary Indian cinema. It is a sophisticated—yes, a highly sophisticated—message, and its moral is despair, for it offers a cosmic impotence as the domain of human existence, with only vicarious and gratuitous vengeance as an individualistic release valve. There is nothing anyone can do about larger issues, for there is nothing anyone can do about anything—beyond kick the one villain you can see in the face.

British Asians, with their particular need to forge a new identity for themselves—one that is rooted in the traditions of India, but which is at the same time totally contemporary and observably British—have been trapped by the formulaic mythology of modern Indian cinema. To be 'Asian' is to be like Vijay/Amitab, aggressively individualistic, or the eternally suffering and obsessive 'Ma' with a suffocating idealised notion of a close-knit family/community; to be modern is to dress in the latest fashion and grace the discos. The metaphysics of the Amitabh and post-Amitabh films has been internalised by a whole generation of Asians who have known little of the Subcontinent except what they have seen on the endlessly grinding and over-used video machines. Not surprisingly, their perceptions of themselves, other Asian communities, tradition and issues of identity and culture are as anodyne as those of today's Indian cinema. It is their bag and baggage, it gives them the identikit outlook to stand up for themselves—but no cogent idea of what to stand for or against. Impotence is a package deal that come with the territory and character notes of the savvy, worldly-wise and somewhat jaded action man; it is his cosmic essence—despite all the kicks and happenstance setting things to rights that is each particular story. Before the forces that define existence he can do nothing, for there is nothing to do about anything larger than your individual lot.

In India, as Javed Akhtar, the writer of *Sholay* and other Amitab Bachchan films, has observed, the Hindi commercial cinema serves as one of 'the strongest binding forces in the country'; it has become 'the common language' of the nation. In Britain, the Indian cinema has sown the seeds of discord and fissures within the Asian community and denied it the possibility of developing a common language of self-description and the evolution of new symbols and ideals that could serve as signposts towards shaping a new identity. It has trapped the British Asian consciousness within a cycle of formulaic conventions that serve as a substitute for genuine, dynamic tradition and ease the pain and frustrations of a loss of belonging. The cyclical retellings offer no possibility of a new kind of becoming, a means towards a new vision of the past, present or future. A community that can only articulate the nature of its own perplexity through the formulas of pot-boiling melodrama and hear it all said for them in meaningless lyrics of rent-a-tune songs is a lobotomised community. It has not only reduced its historic, cultural and personal identity to an absurdity, diminished its art and language, but also abandoned the pursuit of great ideas. Sunrise will find the same audience as benighted in a week or a year or a decade. The identification of the Self with Indian cinema works and makes money because, for a large segment of the Asian community, that's all there is. The stream of hysteric advertisements on Sunrise radio for Sunrise-sponsored 'extravaganzas' to see, hear, touch and meet 'your favourite stars', most notably Amitabh Bachchan—'the Shanshah (king of kings) of Indian film industry', 'the nobility of stoicism', 'the implacability against inexhaustible evil'—are based on an understanding of the allure of the only point of glamour, the dark sepulchre of the cinema, in otherwise humdrum lives. Like the films, on Sunrise radio, as in the Asian community itself, the only development of the plot is the increasing complexity of irrelevant detail, as the pattern goes on replicating itself in ever minute detail while everything stays the same.

VII

On my fortieth birthday, my mother (Ma!), a devoted Muslim, decided to throw a surprise party. Throughout my life, Ma's best friends have always been Hindu, and for the last decade it has been Surita. Surita is not just her best friend but also her neighbour—which means that she has more rights than all of our distant, and not-so-distant, relatives put together. Nothing important happens in our family without Surita's involvement. Even though there are good twenty years between them, the two women are joined by some primordial umbilical cord: always together, always concerned about, and looking after, each other's needs, always cooking special dishes for each other (the *fatiha kheer* and sweetmeats going from here, the *puja alu puri* and *baturas* coming the other way), always sowing *joras* (traditional suits) for each other—and, not infrequently, standing up to the chauvinism of each other's more than traditional husbands. The surprise was the arrival of Surita's mother.

This was Surita's mother's first visit to England—indeed, her very first excursion outside India. My mother had gathered the whole family to receive and welcome her. Surita's mother (of indeterminate age past seventy) arrived and greeted my mother as though she was her daughter who she had not seen for decades but who had kept her well informed and abreast of developments. After initial introductions and courtesies, the three women, ignoring the rest of the two families, started talking animatedly of times past, of Hindustan, of Partition, of separation, migration and transformations. Feeling somewhat ignored, my father interrupted the conversation. 'There will be plenty of time for all the reminiscence,' he said, 'tell us what would you like to see? We must make full use of the time you will spend with us in London.' Surita's mother looked straight at my father. 'Bhai,' she replied reflectively, 'I have come here to do only two things. I am with my two daughters and want to spend all my time in their company. And I want to see as many Pakistani dramas as it is possible to see during the short while I am in London.' Then turning to my mother she asked: 'What do you have in stock?'

Surita's mother stayed six months with her 'two daughters'. Virtually all that time, day and night, the three women confined themselves to Surita's living room. Curtains partially drawn, trays dripping sweetmeats and overflowing savouries on the coffee table, a never-ending supply of tea and pan (betel leaf) punctuated with sachets of 'Shahi Supari' (a mixture of betel nuts and aniseed), they sat in front of the video watching 13-hour long Pakistani television dramas. I asked Surita's Ma what was it that she liked about these dramas. Without a moment's thought she replied: '*Zaban*' (language). Then she thought for a moment and added: 'and stories'.

Both the language and contents of Pakistani television dramas—these are real dramas, not soap operas—echo the essence of the classical films of Dilip Kumar and Guru Dutt. Socially relevant stories, often popping straight out of current affairs, are acted out with style, grace and with a literary language that deliberately diffuses the boundary between dialogue and poetry. There are no songs, no dances, no obligatory fight scenes, no separation of brothers/friends during childhood, no inevitable growth into a mean fighting machine, no ever-present, possessive Ma, no formulas, just serious, humanistic explorations of contemporary social and political issues that challenge both the established oppressive mores as well as alienating but fashionable modernity. Despite being the products of an allegedly 'Islamic state', these dramas have no sectarian religious content. Just as in *Gunga Jumna* and *Pyassa*, what is important is not the religious persuasion of the characters but their internal contradictions and struggle against a socially and politically unjust world. In other words, Pakistani dramas are about the Subcontinent and its struggle to shape a contemporary identity.

How the Subcontinent is changing and not changing, what forces are propelling it towards shaping a new identity and what is holding it back, was powerfully explored in the big hit of the nineties, *Chand Girhan* (Lunar Eclipse). *Chand Girhan*, a fourteen-part state-of-the-nation play by Asghar Nadim Sayed, is about Pakistan, but much of what it has to say is equally applicable to India, Bangladesh and Sri Lanka. Lal Hussain Shah, a Sindhi feudal landlord, loses his seat in the general election. The very peasants whose life he holds in his hands have refused to vote for him. 'It is not food that the peasants want today,' he tells his son, Jahanyar Shah, 'but respect and dignity'. The experience changes Shah 'Sciene' (as Sindhi feudal lords are known) and he genuinely begins to regard and treat the peasants with esteem and decency. In the realist world of Pakistani dramas, when characters learn from their mistakes they do not become instant beacons of goodness—as in Indian films—but struggle to transcend their weaknesses. Shah Sciene wants to change with time and win back the hearts of the peasants who till his land, but he wants the feudal system to move forward unhindered. Jhanyar

Shah, on the other hand, believes in the old method of coercion. 'In this land, even a bird cannot flap her wings without our permission,' he says repeatedly—how dare the peasants vote for the opposition: 'Wven after sprouting wings, ants remain ants and can still be trampled under one's feet.' Jahanyar goes on a mission of revenge and kills three peasants who insist that their votes are a matter for their conscience not the right of the landlord or a commodity for sale.

Shah Sciene is thus faced with two tasks: he has to save his son from the gallows as well as regain his parliamentary seat. But the election defeat has also reduced his power and influence; to accomplish both tasks he must rebuild his powerbase. In Shahyar Bano, his London-educated daughter, he sees a way back to parliament. Bano is in love with Nasir, son of the newspaper owner, Kamal Hasan. But Nasir's father does not command the social status and political influence that Shah Sciene requires. 'If you are caught in the rain,' Shah Sciene tells Bano, 'you have to seek shelter. And if you can't find anywhere to hide from the rain, you try and cover your head with your hands.' An alliance with Babar, a high-ranking civil servant, would provide the kind of shelter that Shah Sciene needs. He thus forces Bano to marry Babar's son, Amjad. Babar himself is using his son as an investment in the future. He needs political backing to realise his ambition to become an industrialist.

But in today's Pakistan, the alliance of feudalism and bureaucracy is not enough to ensure success: the old powerbrokers need the new image maker—the press. Both Shah Sciene and Babar want to buy the backing of Kamal Hasan, and Kamal is only too willing to oblige. 'News is not what happens,' Kamal tells his son, Nasir, 'news is what is made to happen.' Nasir, only too aware of what is happening in the country, wants to report the truth, he wants to expose the corruption of high office and highlight the plight of the unemployed youth. Whereas Babar corrupts his idealist son Amjad, Nasir transforms his corrupt father, Kamal—even though Kamal continues to harbour the tendency of reverting back to appeasing the powerful. Both discover the power the press has to usher in genuine change.

Shahyar Bano refuses to be a conventional, submissive wife and her marriage to Amjad ends in divorce. The alliance of Babar and Shah Sciene is broken and Babar seeks revenge by exposing the feudal landlord. Jahanyar, hiding in the jungle with a well-known robber, kidnaps Babar. Shah Sciene tries to make a deal with the government and the police, but without political clout he is easily outmanoeuvred. Jahanyar and his companion are shot.

Running parallel to the main theme of a feudal landlord coping with change are a number of sub-plots. It is a common practice for the feudal landlords in the Subcontinent to keep a second wife in the city. In Shah Sciene's case it is Gulbahr, a former singer of ill-repute, who discovers that, in today's world, singing on television is a better route to respectability than marrying a feudal lord. There is the story of Amirun Nisa, a Bangladeshi housewife, who arrives in Pakistan looking for employment, but ends up being kidnapped and sold into prostitution.

Like most Pakistani television serials, *Chand Girhan* runs for an astounding twelve hours, during which the characters are fleshed out in the minutest detail. Both Shah Sciene and Jahanyar are complex figures coping, or refusing to cope with, change on their own terms. Like his father, Jahanyar has also married secretly—but he has married a peasant woman that his father refuses to accept. Shah Sciene wants peasants to be treated with respect and dignity but kept at an arm's length; Jahanyar wants to be with them and is perplexed by their disloyalty. It is only Babar, the high-ranking bureaucrat, who refuses to change. As a result of his feud with Shah Sciene, he loses his job, and along with it all the concessions and favours he has gained to establish his industry. He simply finds another, even more powerful, family for his son to marry in. 'The truth is that now people like us can only survive like this. We need them; they need us,' he tells his wife.

In the end, Shah Sciene wins his parliamentary seat back and becomes a government minister. But who has won and who has lost? Shah Sciene is not so sure. 'You have won by sacrificing your son,' Bano tells him. But Shah Sciene is concerned with genealogy: neither his son with Gulbahr or his grandson, the child of a peasant woman, can take his place. 'You don't understand,' he explains. 'I will give them all the respect and rights that are due to them. But they cannot take over the chair I am sitting on: the system will not accept it.' Bano replies: 'But the system is created by people like you. If you can change, the system can change too.' And Shah Sciene goes through another change: he agrees to brush conventions asides and let Bano marry Nasir.

Through a powerfully contemporary narrative, acted with equal power and panache, *Chand Girhan* argues that, despite all the odds, gradual change is possible. Shah 'Seince' is no Thakur—the total personification of all evil—but the victim of a system that has been created by people like him. He is changing—but he cannot change instantaneously. 'Why is it', Bano asks him at the beginning of the play, 'that you recognise the rights of your peasant voters to choose, but you cannot give the same right to your daughter?' By the end of the narrative, Shah Sciene is willing to recognise Bano's rights too. But the viewers have also changed: by engaging with a play that refuses to compromise and offer easy solutions, they have learnt that it is possible to dent the system—viable change will come from guarded optimism, rather than angry and vengeful pessimism. The current problems are like the eclipse of the moon—they can be overcome to reveal the true face of the Subcontinent.

In *Chand Girhan*, both Bano and Gulbahr refuse to be passive victims. Pakistani dramas are full of fiercely independent women, like *Gunga Jumna's* Dhunno, who frequently stand up to oppressive convention and are not afraid to struggle alone. While traditional, they are hardly dependent on their men; while modern, they are constantly questioning the accepted definitions of modernity, and trying to transcend them, in order to discover a modernity that is rooted in their tradition. In *Uroosa*, for example, Anjum, the wife of a famous lawyer, refuses to be victimised by his sisters and his neglect. *She* divorces *him*—a situation unheard of in the Indian cinema. Divorced, Anjum not only brings up her daughter, Uroosa, but returns to the University for further education. After struggling through several episodes, Anjum herself becomes a lawyer. At the end of the play, it is her ex-husband who comes crawling back. In Tanhaiyan, Zahra, the elder daughter of a famous film producer who is killed in an accident, struggles alone to repossess the dream house of her father. She starts a business and, in the course of events, acquires a business partner as well as a lover, succeeding against all odds. But the goals of her efforts produce the same loneliness that she felt under the shadow of her father—the '*Tanhaiyan*' of the title. The dream house is as empty as the materialism which led her parents to neglect her. Even when the women are not the main focus of the story, they are portrayed as thinking individuals trying to stand up to both traditional and modern chauvinism. In *Lakeerain*, a complicated play about the Pathans of the North West frontier, the young geologist, Mureed, is up against the combined might of the devious Mir Sahab, the village landlord, and Sait Jabbar, a city businessman. The main narrative is concerned with Mureed's efforts to excavate the mineral deposits in the village for the benefit of his villagers and stop Mir and Jabbar laying their greedy hands on the hidden riches of the village. However, all the women in the play—Natasha, the educated daughter of Jabbar; Faryal, who has studied medicine and is the daughter of Karam Khan, Mir's sidekick; and Nazo, the daughter of a blind villager—are shown fighting oppression in their own individual way. Nazo makes rugs and pots for her blind father to sell; she loves Mureed and finally gets her man. Natasha defies her father to marry according to her own wish, and when her husband turns out to be a scoundrel, leaves him without hesitation. She supports Mir against her father's partner and declares: 'I respect you Uncle, but that does not mean I am here to obey you.' Faryal fights to practise medicine and in the end achieves her goal. All this despite the fact that they are confined, not just within the four walls of their house, but also by a tradition they are trying to change. The world of Pakistani drama is not so much the world of Mother India but the Subcontinent of wives, daughters and sisters, struggling, seeking, forging a new identity for themselves. Not surprisingly, many of the plays of Pakistani television are written by established women writers.

The role of tradition in shaping a contemporary identity is a constant theme in Pakistani serials. In *Khawaja and Son*, a comedy of traditional manners in twelve episodes by Ata Ullah Qasmi, the place of tradition in Pakistani society is explored with loving detail. Khawaja Feroze, a widowed, retired teacher, is the traditional father of nine daughters. The eldest daughter, Fazilat, has cracked under the pressure of bringing up her younger sisters and is in a psychiatric hospital. Six other daughters have been married and Khawaja now lives with the two youngest, Samina and Assiya, and his only son, Jawadad. The family live in the old part of Lahore with its labyrinthine alleys, closed courtyards, extended families; a part of the city where even the shoeshine man is more than a personal friend. Jawadad is a successful and well known poet who works at a government publishing house. He dreams of marrying Yasmine, his college sweetheart, despite the fact that Yasmine's rich, businessman father, A.W. Chaudhry, has already rejected his proposal. His daily agenda is full with the problems of the family: on a typical day he has to take his father to visit his hospitalised sister, find a job for the son of his sister Rabia, reconcile the differences between his sister Razia and her husband. As a respected poet, he is constantly in demand for *mushairas*, appears on television, and is perpetually plagued by mediocre and aspiring poets seeking his literary favours. His boss, Professor Allah Ditta, who writes under the pen name of 'Udas' (the Sad One) and has delusions of being a poet, is jealous of his success and takes every opportunity to make his life difficult. He is also the subject of constant attentions from his neighbour, Nabila, a simple, traditional girl who has problems pronouncing her r's. Nabila loves Jawadad and, in her innocence, often asks him to explain the meaning of saucy verses.

The main theme of *Khawaja and Son* is the relationship, within an extended family, between father and son. Khawaja may be a traditional father but he is not a blind follower of tradition: he uses humour as his weapon both to demolish suffocating tradition and to keep isolating modernity at bay. For him, tradition is based on unconditional love that not just binds his family but hold the community together. He doesn't want sacrifices; only that people relate to each other 'with open heart'. He goes on a weekly round of visits to all his daughters and insists that his son spends some time in idle chit-chat with his sisters. Only by open and free flow of conversation can the dirt of suspicion be cleansed from the heart. And Khawaja and Jawadad talk not just as father and son but as lifelong pals, as equals, as confidants. When Khawaja discovers that Jawadad has been seeing Yasmine, he tells his son, 'I am not just your father but also your best friend. Don't hide anything from me. I will complain. Right? That girl Yasmine is still on your mind?' Jawadad changes the subject: 'Oh please! Listen to me: marry Samina.' Khawaja laughs at his son's manoeuvre. Jawadad then comes back with a verse:

> Jawadad: Abu, the duration of one's journey determines the luggage one carries.

Khawaja: Yes. Yes. Yes. I see. My son is about to receive a poetic revelation from the sky. Here—hold this pen. I will keep cups of tea flowing every five minutes. A *ghazal* should be ready in about twenty minutes.

Jawadad: Abu—I am not talking about the poetry of love but the poetic justice of everyday life.

Khawaja: And what is that?

Jawadad: You know the marital problems of Razia. You have seen what has happened to Fazilat. Please do not give so much love to your daughters. They will always find their husbands wanting in this regard. Without that much love they will see their own houses as deserts—as hell.

Khawaja: My own house is a paradise. A garden whose beauty is enhanced by the presence of my daughters who are like a flock of birds. What is a garden without birds? An oasis without water?

Jawadad: I am not saying all this because I am tired of my sisters. No. Sisters are like a cool shadow on a scorching day.

Khawaja admits to making mistakes but he sees his unconditional love for his children as a liberating force. For him, tradition and reflection go hand in hand and both are bound by a warm humanity. Not surprisingly, he agrees both to marry Samina to Jawadad's friend Zahid—he knows that they love each other—and to try, yet again, to persuade Chaudhry to give his daughter's hand in marriage to Jawadad.

Jawadad represents the transformation of tradition within tradition. He is a traditional man without being suffocated by it; he is a modern man without being alienated by modernity. When his friend Zahid asks him to leave the problems of his sisters behind and go to America, he is appalled by the suggestion. His sisters, his father, are the source of his happiness. 'I have been to America on poetry recitals', he says. 'I have seen our expatriate

Pakistanis; I have talked to them. Their entire life revolves around a few plastic credit cards in their pockets which buy them worldly comforts but take away their happiness as interest. Strapped in their seatbelts, they drive their big cars on the highway—their entire life is spent unsuccessfully looking for the exits.' Zahid's own flirtation with modernity (he dresses like Abitab Buchchan and goes out with girls) has not only alienated him from the girl he loves (Jawadad's sister Samina) but also from his own mother. But Zahid is not an unthinking man—like Shashi Kapoor in so many Indian films, returning home from US/Europe, a woman in each arm, a guitar round the shoulder, whose liberation comes simply by learning to say 'mummy darling'. He constantly questions his own motives and seeks meaning in his life.

The women too are just as reflective and assertive. Razia gives as good as she gets from her greedy husband Ludan. Nabila pursues her love interest with uncanny vigour, popping up at every opportune moment. Samina wants her future husband to live up to her expectations of decency. When Zahid's mother tells Samina that her beauty should not be hidden behind a veil, she snaps back: 'true beauty is diminished by exhibition'. Zahid's mother has herself thought about tradition and modernity. After visting Khawaja and his family, she tells Samina: 'I like the old city very much. It looks like people here have been glued together by love. Where we live—those places are beautiful only to look at. But there, beauty is like the beauty of white man's graveyard.' Samina is troubled with this romantic view of tradition. 'But the old city is brimming with its own problems,' she says. 'Yes,' Zahid's mother replies, 'I know they too have problems.' Then she trunactes the Urdu word for problems—*masaial* to *saial*—and transforms its meaning. 'But problems which permit human beings to retain their humanity are not problems but questions that beg viable answers.'

A PERSON OF PAKISTANI ORIGINS

While Khawaja and Jawadat present the liberating face of tradition, Chaudhry, who adds an 'n' to every word he utters and describes himself as 'a very modern and very liberal man', uses tradition to advance his materialistic goals. He tells Yasmine that tradition requires that she marries a man with a similar financial standing to her father. It is a question of respect. What has Jawadad got, he asks Yasmine—and answers the question himself: 'An old house in Bhatti gate. A scooter he won in the lottery. And yes: that job as a deputy director. My secretary is paid more than him.' When Yasmine replies that he is 'one of our most popular and respected poets', Chaudhry retorts: 'Is that a qualification to marry in wealth? Have you seen the matrimonial ads in the newspaper? They clearly and categorically state that poets need not apply as rejection often offends.' Yasmine, who 'moves in the fast lane', is eventually forced to abandon her father and runs away to Canada.

Without ducking difficult issues, *Khawaja and Son* explores the joys and problems of extended families with biting humour and a loving, embracing eye. Professor Udas adds a sentence to a government textbook comparing himself to the classic poets Ghalib, Mir and Iqbal, and consequently loses his job. Zahid abandons the quest of meaningless modernity and marries Samina. Khawaja fakes a heart attack and persuades Jawadad to look beyond Nabila's simplicity. 'Shall I tell you something straight from my heart?' he asks his son: 'Never trust people like A W Chaudhry who have pulled their roots from the ground and covered their faces with the mud of (westernised) pride. My son, Nabila is a good woman. These people have their roots very deep in the soil, very deep.' Jawadad finally explains the meaning of that verse about the lovers' consummation of their desire to Nebila.

Tradition is often blamed for individuals' and society's own failures. Indeed, in the Subcontinent there is a tradition of blaming everyone and everything for one's own weaknesses and shortcomings. Anwar Masood's *Aangan Tehra*, written in a delicious Punjabised Urdu, explores both the notions of failure as well as the tradition of putting the blame elsewhere. The play takes its title from the Urdu proverb *Natch na Jane, aangan tehra*. Literary, the proverb relates to dancers who cannot dance but blame the unevenness of the dance floor, or more specifically, the veranda or courtyard (*aangan*) where they would traditionally dance. Mahboob Ahmad, the protagonist of the narrative, is a childless civil servant who has been unceremoniously retired before his time. Mahboob's failure lies in his honesty and integrity. His wife, Jahan Ara, a lovable but cynical women, constantly chides him for being too honest by half. The couple have been lumbered with Akbar, a homosexual classical dancer who 'walks like an air hostess', is unable, as well as unwilling, to work as a dancer and has become their servant. Akbar has not been paid for three years and refuses to leave without his pay—which, given the couple's state of poverty, means that he is a permanent member of the family. The ideas of failure in a society that places success at a high premium are explored by a constant and aggressive wordplay between Akbar and Jahan Ara, much of it generated by Akbar's domination of the kitchen, and an equally dynamic but gentler wordplay between Jahan Ara and Mahboob. Much of the wordplay—a constant feature of Pakistani television dramas—also serves as social and political comment. When Mahbood decides to stand for local council elections, Jahan Ara uses the occasion to highlight Mahboob's past failures: 'You can't even sit (on a job), how are you going to stand for an election?' When Akbar brings in the shopping, Jahan Ara demands: 'Why can't you buy fresh potatoes?' 'Because,' Akbar replies, 'they have all been exported to the Gulf.' 'Whatever for?' Jahan Ara is perplexed. 'So that we can import crisps from Europe,' Akbar flashes back.

Whereas Mahboob is a failure, his Punjabi neighbour Chaudry Dalat Ali Khan, who lives with his unmarried sister Sultana, is a successful landowner and businessmen. Jahan Ara is impressed by Chaudhry's success, even though she knows that it is the result of less than honest dealings. Chaudhry, wanting Mahboob to win the local Council election so that as Councillor Mahbood could award him new licences to expand his business, arranges for Mahboob to return uncontested. But Mahboob is not interested in a manoeuvred success that forces him to oblige Chaudhry with extra business. He tricks Chaudhry into becoming the Councillor.

Unable to meet their bills, Mahboob and Jahan Ara decide to rent part of the house. Along come a series of paying guests—a journalist, a poet, an actor, a policeman—all of whom have tried, but ultimately failed in their vocations. The couple end up paying for their upkeep. The journalist blames the fall in readership of his paper for his failure; the poet blames his failure on the fact that even though he always speaks the truth no one listens to him; the actor on the VCR. What is the point of education, creativity and hard work when they cannot guarantee material success, Jahan Ara wonders: 'I have an educated husband, a creative servant, even my paying guests are educated? But there is not even four annas in the house!' Still, says Lahri—a real and failed Pakistani comedian playing a failed Pakistani comedian seeking to recharge his batteries at the couple's house—there is the compensation of the VCR. Whenever we feel too depressed by our own failures, we can just press the button and have 'the Westerners dancing at our whims'.

Aangan Tehra 'is a sharply observed, highly sophisticated play that pulls few punches. When the couple are forced to sell their furniture, we witness the gradual transformation of Jahan Ara as she begins to question her criteria for measuring success. But her transformation does not change her character: she simply learns to adjust to her declining level of poverty and the acidic wordplay continues. In the penultimate, twelfth episode, the writer, Asad Masood, script in hand walks onto the set and declares that he too has failed to develop his characters beyond familiar stereotypes. But the play has been very successful: 'I am very popular,' says Chaudhry. Nevertheless, the writer collects his characters, Akbar, Chaudry and Sultana, and drives them off the set. In the final episode, we meet Mahboob and Jahan Ara twenty years later. They are visited by a young, failed burglar: failed because he only got third division in the BA final, 'one result produced the other', and because he chooses a poverty stricken house to rob. The couple treat him in exactly the same way as they treated all those failed 'paying guests' they entertained earlier: with concern, dignity and a sharp tongue. The young thief is forced to confront his failure: how can I go on blaming others for what is ultimately my own weakness?

It is possible to describe *Aangan Tehra* as a postmodern narrative. It has all the familiar traits: wordplay, entertaining mixing of real and imaginary characters, a highly self-conscious intervention by the writer himself, ethnic and sexual plurality and ambiguity... But that would be to pigeonhole *Aangan Tehra* into a current Western fad. Like its characters, *Aangan Tehra* has deeply traditional roots. Wordplay, ethnic plurality and other features of postmodernism have been regular fare of Urdu literature for decades, if not centuries. Indeed, the basic concerns of postmodern novels, as popularised by Salman Rushdie amongst others, 'the experience of uprooting, disjuncture and metamorphosis', have appeared in the Urdu novel since the partition of the Subcontinent.

Not surprisingly, Pakistani television dramas have followed suit. Issues of uprooting, disjuncture and identity have been tackled head-on in numerous plays, some of which have been brought together in long running television series under a general theme. In the seventies, *Coffee House* explored the issues of rural displacement and questions of rural and urban identity. The eighties hit *Airport* explores the issues of migration and metamorphosis in a series of one-hour plays of stunning brilliance. In one episode of *Airport*, a young Pakistani girl, who has been brought up in Virginia, USA, returns with her parents to Karachi. She left a traditional girl, but now she returns as a modern woman: she is interested in pop music, English literature, Kung Fu fighting and has difficulty with her Urdu. She is immediately surrounded by her uncles and aunts, each with a son in toe, all wooing her to become their daughter-in-law. Horrified, intrigued and amused in turn, she decides to play along. She discovers that all the eligible bachelors she meets are willing to change themselves according to her wishes. Indeed, a few of them embark on a strict regime of education, musical appreciation and Judo to meet her requirements. Then, on a farm, she meets an agricultural scientist, who not only rejects her advances, but refuses to change his identity. Modernity and tradition are not cloths, he tells her, that one can change into at the slight of hand. You want me to become insane like the others? There are other ways of being modern which have nothing to do with pop music, literary fashion and stylised violence: the quest for that modernity begins here at the farm, in the village, in the rural enclaves of Pakistan. She invites him to go to America with her; he invites her to rediscover her true self. Eventually the girl begins a new metamorphosis: she marries the agricultural scientist and decides to change herself, as well as Pakistan.

Migration does not always modernise those who migrate; neither are the choices between modernity and tradition straightforward. In another episode of *Airport*, a young doctor returns to Pakistan after six years of medical training; she is horrified by the American lifestyle and has become even more determined to maintain her tradition. While in the US, she adopted an orphaned child of Pakistani expatriates; in Pakistan she is forced to confront her husband's prejudice against child adoption. When forced with a choice between keeping the husband or the child, she takes the untraditional option and abandons the husband.

The adopted son grows up to realise that he is an American citizen, and is himself faced with the choice of migrating to the US and a secured heritage, abandoning the women who brought him up, or staying with her and struggling in Pakistan. He chooses to abandon her in favour of the US. Another episode of *Airport* explores the effects of migration on those who are left behind. A young executive returns from the Gulf with a suitcase full of expensive gifts for relatives and friends. The airline loses his suitcase and he is unable to fulfill their expectations of his success abroad. Slowly, he realises that his migration has transformed his family and friends: whereas before they related to him as he was, now they can only relate to him through their transformed expectations of his success. Even his wife is transformed; only he remains unchanged!

Like the classic Indian cinema of Dilip Kumar and Guru Dutt, Pakistani drama is dominated by literary figures who not only understand the power of art and literature but are actually using it to reshape society and develop a new identity for Pakistan. It is difficult to see a Pakistani drama and not be engaged by it: they force the viewers to think, question themselves and raise questions about meaning and the meaning of modernity, about tradition and traditional identity, about change and changing—and they do all this without any sex and violence. It is not art for art's sake, but art that seeks to transform and transcend society for its sake. In Britain, they could become the entertainment balm that heal the wounds of suspicion and fragmentation.

VIII

Today, it isn't my birthday: just an ordinary Sunday. I started the day with that very British institution, the Sunday newspapers, reading some heavy think pieces on the current hot topic: the relationship between social malaise and the cinema and television. Is Hollywood causing the brutalisation of America through its veneration of violence, ugliness and sexual venality?, asks film critic, Michael Medved. Is television violence leading a younger generation to become mindless criminals? Is unrestrained sexual indulgence and deviance, made normal by constant repetition in the cinema and on television, undermining traditional morality, denigrating everyone's dignity, eroding established values and destroying the family as a viable institution and the bedrock of society? Is cinema, television or the VCR the cause, as the moral crusaders insist, or merely the mirror and messenger of our own shortcomings as the media establishment invariably asserts?

Once again, Dilip Kumar makes me do it. In the cultural debate of western society, of which I am a part because I am a British citizen, I cannot stand aloof. My upbringing in the Walthamstow Cameo and King Cross Scala, as well as my formation through the BBC's once legendary and now somewhat faded mandate to inform, educate and entertain, and membership of the Baby Boom generation that expresses itself through Hollywood films and established the classics of the pop culture—all impelled me to reflection on the issues, arguments and errant insanity and confusion of this vexed debate. The history of Indian cinema in my experience and lifetime has something important to add to the debate about mass international culture, the homogenising globalisation that is going on apace everywhere. When contemporary Indian films surrendered their Indianess, they lost their potency as cultural communication— they made an entire culture inarticulate in the face of both its own tradition and modernity. The cultural formation of contemporary Indian cinema prepares no one to be self-reflective, and without self-reflection and articulacy, how can anyone think their way through the despairing morass of real issues of life? How can the Asians of the Subcontinent be responsible citizens of the globe? Surely our subcontinental debates, problems, issues—our wrestling with tradition and modernity—must have something to offer to the international and global debates about values, decency and the politics of the future? Isn't the cultural production of any society a window on its soul, and doesn't it show what its cherished values have to offer, not just to itself but the world at large? So what exactly is there to choose between Arnold Schwarzenegger and Amitabh Bachchan? Except that Amitabh is the standard-bearer of a new Indian metaphysic that hands control of the world to Arnie—'hasta la vista baby!', rat tatat, rat tatat, and 'have a nice day'.

I was not having a nice day. The strains of these thoughts were getting as complicated as the plot of an Amitabh potboiler and the detail as confused and hard to hold onto. Somewhere in this labyrinthine web of interconnections I was missing the hooks and footholds that would lead to some solid conclusions about an appropriate active response. I was about ready to throw my hands in despair when the doorbell rang. My friend Arun and his wife Indu arrived with a bottle of garlic pickle that Indu's auntie had sent from India. I met Arun during my days at London Weekend Television where he used to edit my 'Eastern Eye' film reports. Since then Indu has been the best friend of my wife: they look a bit alike and behave as though they were twin sisters. We chatted for a while and then my wife suggested some entertainment; we watched a couple of episode of *Dast*, a Pakistani drama about rural tradition and identity and how rural Baluchistan is changing. 'How refreshing,' Indu commented after the tape finished, 'to see a film where the hero is not called Vijay and the villain in not Thakur.' Well that did it. Here we were all Asians, citizens of Britain, Muslim and Hindu, two of us media professionals, all parents concerned about our children, the society in which they are growing up, the world in which they live and the future they will inherit. There was a lot more to say, much more to discuss. And we did.

We did not reach any conclusive resolution. The subject, perhaps, requires more sustained and gradual work. But from the complexity and morass of my morning's reflections and impulses, some elements of clear thinking emerged from the night's discussion. The worst of tradition and westernisation are compelling, complicit helpmates, when they come together either in the East or in the West—in Asian culture or Western culture. The result is markedly similar: a message of despair and impotence that degrades society and human dignity; the means and expression can be both similar and distinctly different, the result is ominously uniform.

Pakistani television drama was an important starting point for a thoughtful discussion. It is something refreshing, something resonant and challenging, something distinctively Asian. It makes a nonsense of the hermetic containers into which the subcontinent has isolated itself, making cultural strangers of neighbours. The divisions and fissures in our subcontinental affiliations make us all weaker before the onslaught of westernisation, prevent us from offering mutual sustenance and support in the face of a global battle that centres on values and ideals. In the realm of values and ideals, Asians of the Subcontinent, at home or in Britain, share a common history in which their diverse traditions matured together and which are their strongest bulwark for finding domestic answers to contemporary problems.

Art cannot be divorced from life: the theme of *Mughal-e-Azam*. I keep returning to the formative text of my adolescence. When art becomes the perpetual parody of pastiche, as in contemporary Indian cinema, then something of our reality and potential is diminished. A sophisticated film creates a sophisticated audience. The audience that filled the Walthamstow Cameo and Kings Cross Scala did not cease to exist or simply evaporate into thin air. This audience did not lose its wits overnight, but it did successively and progressively cease to be served by a popular cinema that was

sophisticated and distinctly Indian. Popular culture has a responsibility to society and cultural evaluation. Contemporary Indian
cinema is not the only culpable criminal, but it is guilty of denigrating the cultural excellence that its society can bring forth. It is
less then it should be and we all are diminished by the failure of its
imagination—indeed, it is determined to have no visible brain at
all. In art, the reverse proposition is now real life—a mindless film
cultivates a small-minded audience that loses touch with the high
water mark of its cultural heritage.

Art mirrors life: the argument of *Mughal-e-Azam*. What else
has art to work with? But our reflection, what we see in the
mirror, is not without consequence, even when it is not the sole
and singular cause of any decision we make. When what the
metaphysics of art mirrors back to us is a cosmic condition of
despair and impotence wrapped with sophistication in the mind-
lessness of diverting entertainment, then it is no innocent
bystander. It is part of the problem calling out for change. The
mechanics of popular entertainment are such that society cannot
enforce such change, cannot legislate it, cannot vote with its feet
effectively enough. The professionals hold the power in the
media. If they fail to be responsible to the highest artistic traditions, society can only take what is given, however unsatisfying
it may be. The root of mass escapism is not the only way Indian
cinema could develop or make money. The vibrancy and content
of Pakistani television dramas testifies to that.

Art holds up a mirror to life: the message of *Mughal-e-Azam*.
Today's Indian cinema does indeed provide a partial reflection of
the problems of our existence, a reflection of what our history
and modern experience have made us into. But art qualifies as art
when the mirror is a self-reflective device that thinks and feels
and engages its audience in a cultural communication to which it
provides a critical edge, a purchase—the hooks and footholds for
moving forward by qualitative improvement. Contemporary

Indian cinema is only one symptom of how the societies of the Subcontinent have lost their way in the modern world. Pakistani television plays seem to argue that popular entertainment can be one ingredient in helping to find our way out of the mess we have created for ourselves.

The great film texts of my youth instilled in me the idea of unconditional love. India, my India, is still a fitting object for such feeling. British Asians of my generation and the generations after me have lost touch with my India, just as India too has diverged from us by seeking to become more like our western domicile. But our identity can never deny that unconditional love for India, my own India, India of the multiplex—the multicultural, the multi-religious world of many traditions living together with an open heart. 'Only by open and free flow of conversation can the dirt of suspicion be cleansed from the heart,' says the old, traditional protagonist of *Khawaja and Son*. Only by the free flow of cultural communication with an open heart can our minds be alerted to what we yet share, how we can yet recover the creativity and cultural resistance we need to withstand the corrosive forces of dehumanising and depersonalising homogenisation on a global scale. Only in our modern predicament and traditional culture can we find the point of balance to change ourselves and the world in which we live. Mindful of both poles that move us, Asians have something very unique to offer to today's debates, the debates that fill my Sunday papers. So few British Asians or voices of the subcontinent are internationalist because of this failure to achieve our own multicultural point of mutual balance and communication. If we cannot make it work— as a subcontinent that binds and roots so many different and interlinked cultures and histories—how could we expect the rest of the world to be the plural and open setting we need to have our own identity and be at home wherever we live?

We talked quite late into the night. We did not agree about everything but we all felt better, felt positive, felt we had found some important and missing common ground through our discussion. As Indu was leaving she remarked that she hoped we would like the pickle, 'and can I borrow the tape of the conclusion of that series?' I fell asleep with a vision of the smiling faces of Dilip Kumar and Guru Dutt swimming into my head.

5.

········

LOVE, DEATH AND URDU POETRY

········

I

A few minutes after 9pm, on 12 May 1978, the compound of the Pakistani embassy in Jeddah, Saudi Arabia, started to reverberate to the sounds of 'wah', 'wah'—wonderful, superb, brilliant, stunning! It was an unbearably hot evening. Over a thousand people, crammed into a small veranda designed originally to accommodate no more than a few hundred, sweated and swayed in unison to the rhyme and rhythm, sounds and inspirations, of Urdu poetry.

An evening of poetry at an embassy on foreign soil suggests an elitist gathering where the notable and worthy, the great and the good, submit to an exercise in polite boredom devised purely to promote national image. Nothing could be further from the truth. Apart from the fact I was there—and neither then nor since has anyone considered me elite—this was a Pakistani *mushaira*. The institution is distinctive, specific and yet protean. It is an occasion for appreciation of artistry that rises to esoteric exuberance, accompanied with overtones of the partisan allegiances of a football crowd chanting their anthems, supporting their heroes, proclaiming their loyalties, intoxicated with the skill, the verve, of the players, urging them on with abandon—a crowd relishing every moment. They are experiencing exactly what Bill Shankly, Grand Master of Liverpool FC, once explained is 'not a matter of life and death—it's more important than that'. A *mushaira* is the expression of 'Pakistaniness', in all the ambiguity of its existences, precisely because it is not 'Pakistani' at all. And yet—every time I attend a *mushaira* I feel confirmed in my being of Pakistani origins. I was there in my element that night because this is what I was raised to be—a drop in the elemental ocean of belonging that is my heritage and that united me with those who attended and adhere to such heritage. But what is the heritage? That is the question!

It all begins with words. No, that can't be right. It all begins with thought. I suppose so. Anyway, there has to be thought and words, wonderful words that conjure, console, that transport you, invigorate you, inspire you, make you sad and reflective, that traumatise you, fill you with a sense of loss, of love, of longing, of all human life and more. All I know is that I begin with Urdu poetry. It is the source, the wellspring of needing words and ideas as the bedrock of my existence. It is the origin of that exuberance and excitement I find in conversation, in wrestling with concepts, motives, meanings, the things that give living its relevance and resonance. And fun—never forget the sheer delight that can be found in the well-turned phrase, the apposite obser-vation, the playful puncturing of pretension. All this and so much more was instilled in me through the medium of Urdu poetry and I came to know Urdu poetry by attending *mushairas* from my earliest years.

The embassy's *mushaira* began with local poets. A string of individuals who wrote poetry as a hobby appeared on the stage. Some were clearly no more than amateur and drew appropriate responses from the crowd. With the appearance of Waheeda Naseem (d.1996), the recital changed gear:

> *I am still a stranger in my own home*
> *People ask: you, what are you doing here?*

She was followed by the more established poets who had flown in from Pakistan for the occasion—each had to be almost wres-tled away from the crowd. Then Mahir al-Qadri (d. 1978) was invited to present his *kalam*. Now this is one of the tell-tale hall-marks of the culture. In simple terms, Mahir was being asked to take the stage and recite his verse. *Kalam*, however, is no simple word. It is the term for philosophy, so in one elegant word the signal was given that here was a master of the craft and his craft had depth, profundity, a stance, a take on life, the universe, and everything. You see what I mean about the significance of words—it was more than etiquette, more than a flowery introduction it was an earned accolade that invited Mahir to the stage.

Mahir al-Qadri started his literary career after finishing high school; he was the editor of a Karachi-based literary magazine, *Faaraan*. Widely known both for his humorous verse and as a sympathiser of the Jamaat-i-Islami, he established and ran 'Halqa-i-adab-i-Islami', an Islamic literary circle. On this occasion, he was sitting next to another literary lion, Hafeez Jallundhri, who wrote the national anthem of Pakistan. Like Mahir al-Qadri, Hafeez Jallundhri too was not formally educated: he studied in a mosque and left school before he reached his teens. He was the author of *Shahnam-e-Islam*, a history of Islam in verse, and the famous poem, 'I am still young', first sung by Malika Pukhraj in the 1950s and still popular with the senior tendency in Pakistan. Both Mahir al-Qadri and Hafeez Jallundhri (d. 1982) were religious individuals but with different inclinations. Mahir al-Qadri was a legal moralist; every article or poem that was published in *Faaraan* had to conform to an established standard of morality. Misuse of language, a wrong word in the wrong place, was not tolerated; neither were lapses in the norms and conventions of Urdu poetry. *Faaraan* did not publish any pictures (deemed by Mahir al-Qadri as unlawful in Islam). In contrast, Hafeez Jallundhri leaned towards mysticism. He became a disciple of Nawab Uddin Ramdasi, an Indian Sufi scholar and preacher, during his teens. He visited shrines of saints and, according to some, actually sang devotional songs at Sufi gatherings. It was clear to the audience that the two poets were having an animated conversation.

175

A PERSON OF PAKISTANI ORIGINS

As Mahir al-Qadri stood up to recite, the audience began to chant: *'Jamna ka kinaray'*, *'Jamna ka kinaray'* ('by the banks of Jamna'). 'Patience, patience,' Mahir al-Qadri retorted: 'Let me first recite some fresh poems.' He began to recite in *taranum*: that is, he sang (rather than recited) verses whose metre were designed to modulate to musical accompaniment and rendition:

First, bring everything to the same pitch
Then start your heart rendering song
When love reaches its true resonance
It has no eyes for beauty.

After a philosophical meditation on love and beauty, Mahir changed the mood of the crowd and sang some humorous verses. He joked with the audience, complimented them on their etiquette and appreciation of true poetry, and became intoxicated with the atmosphere. He was followed by eighty-year old Hafeez Jallundhri. The audience began chanting *'Abhi tu main jawan hun'*, *'Abhi tu main jawan hun'* ('I am still young'). 'No, no,' Hafeez Jallundhri shouted back waving his arms, 'there will be plenty of time for *that* poem':

Why is the destination so impatient?
I am on my way; I am coming!

After the two literary lions, it was the turn of Ehsan Danish (d. 1982), who was presiding over the *mushaira*. He recited—rather than sang in *taranum*—in a lucid, direct and forceful style. His simple and dignified verses, rising to real eloquence, cast a mystical mood on the gathering. For almost an hour, he mesmerised the audience, turning them into stone. He stood quite motionless on the stage: no movements of the arms, no meaningful gestures of the body. There was solemnity and dignity to his delivery; his verses seemed to flow naturally, almost as though he was talking, a train of thought borne along on his own unique metre. He would emphasise certain words, repeat certain verses, and frequently invite the audience to discover multiple layers of meanings in a particular sonnet.

When love reaches its true resonance
It has no eyes for beauty.
Cold touching hands
Take you to a point from where there is no point.

I was sitting in the front row. As his verses reverberated in my mind, I tried to reconcile what Ehsan Danish had said to me with what he was reciting now. 'A poet lives what he writes', he had said. 'When understanding reaches a certain point, it has no need for life. Live the poems and experience the point beyond which nothing more can be said.'

Even though I had not met him before this visit to Jeddah, I felt I knew Ehsan Danish. During my teenager years, his son, Zeshan Danish, was a regular visitor to our house in East London. He was a leading poet amongst those who regularly attended the monthly *mushairas* my father organised. He talked frequently, and proudly, about his father, who was born into an extremely poor family and was destitute for much of his early life. As a youth, he earned a meagre living by 'acting as an ox' to a landless farmer—literally, he pulled the plough, turned the water wheel and performed other tasks of a beast of burden. He had only two passions: rearing pigeons and writing poetry. Nowadays, Zeshan Danish used to say, it is difficult for someone to get a higher qualification in Urdu without being examined by my father, who never went to school. He gave my father a copy of *Jahan-i-Danish*, the autobiography of his father. My own father forced me to read it, describing it variously as 'a classic' and 'a masterpiece'.

The *mushaira* in Jeddah was meticulously planned. The visiting poets were divided amongst the various members of the expatriate community, who provided hospitality and were responsible for all their needs while they were in Jeddah— including taking them to Mecca to perform the *umra* (the lesser pilgrimage). I lived in Jeddah, working for the Hajj Research Centre, and securing accommodation for Ehsan Danish was a plum assignment, a genuine privilege I was determined to manage. During the 1970s, one of the most prominent Pakistanis in Jeddah was a man called Mohammad Ali. He was the Manager of *Arab News*, a newly launched newspaper. All the Pakistanis, rich and poor, new arrivals as well as those well-established in the city, knew Mohammad Ali. If you needed help—and everyone in Saudi Arabia in those days needed help—you went to Mohammad Ali. And he seldom disappointed anyone. His apartment, on the first floor of Sufi Building in the *balad*, the downtown area, was always open. Complete strangers often walked in and asked for help. At any given time, half a dozen strangers would be sleeping rough in his living room. I spent a great deal of time at his house. He treated me like a younger sibling; I respected and adored him like an older brother. Given the already high rate of eclectic occupancy at his flat he thought it was an inappropriate environment for distinguished guests. I felt otherwise. In the end it proved easy for me to fulfil my objective and persuade him to host Ehsan Danish.

He arrived a day before the *mushaira*. We took him on the obligatory visit to Mecca in the morning and arranged a *mahfil*—a gathering—in the evening. Mohammad Ali had invited a number of what he called *ahl-e-zauq*—folks with an interest in and love of literature. Ehsan Danish sat on a *charpoy* in the living room while we gathered in a circle and sat on the floor around him. The room was closed and the air conditioner turned on to full blast.

Ehsan Danish began the *mahfil* by himself asking a question he was frequently asked: how could someone so totally untutored write poetry? 'Urdu poetry', he said,

> is in our soil and in our souls. You don't have to be formally educated
> to read or write Urdu poetry: it is there all around you, you live in it,

you breathe it. I have no formal schooling, but I am not an uneducated man for poetry has been my tutor. You can learn almost everything, about your Self, your land, your people, your religion, your history, your culture, your nation through the poetry of the classical masters. You don't even have to be able to read for much of it is written to be recited, sung, memorised.

He went on to explain that there are two main forms of Urdu verse: *bayaniyah* (narrative) and *ramziyah* (suggestive). The *masnawi* (versified tale) is one of the major forms of *bayaniyah* verse; it can have as little as ten or twelve or as many as ten thousand verses and is generally composed in seven metres. Virtually all the social and political history of the Indian subcontinent can be found in our *masnawis*. There are religious, historical, social, cultural and patriotic *masnawis*. From the history of the Mughuls to the 1857 Uprising (aka the Indian Mutiny in British historical parlance) to the struggle for independence—'you can learn about them from Urdu verse'. Often major historical events, like the massacre of the Jallianwala Bagh in Amritsar (1919) or the developments in particular areas, have been described in vivid detail in Urdu verse. And how our social customs such as marriage ceremonies and *huqqah* smoking, seasonal and religious celebrations like *Holi* and *Diwali*, have developed and changed—that too, has been chronicled by Urdu verse. Then, of course, there are the great romances. Who in the Punjab does not know, or has not sung, the tragic *masnawi* of Heer Ranjha?

But surely, a professorial type in the assembly insisted, facility with language, the ability to use similes and metaphors, the manipulation of symbolism, the metaphysical or philosophical content—these require some form of high level education. Ehsan Danish laughed; indeed, this was the only time I saw him laugh. 'The forms and convention of the Urdu verse itself teach you these things,' he retorted. 'Look at the *ghazal*, the main form of *ramziyah* verse. Each line in a poem is called a *misra*, and two *misras* make a *shair*. A *ghazal* can consist of anything from five to twenty-five *shairs*. The rhyme can be based on a single word but often it consists of a full phrase. Now, each *shair* must be complete on its own: in other words, the conventions of Urdu poetry dictate that each verse is a poem within a poem. The only formal connection between the *shairs* of a *ghazal* is that of meter and rhyme.' The gathering looked perplexed. Someone asked: but how does that teach you the use of metaphors and symbolism? Anyway, wouldn't the fragmentary quality of the *ghazal* make it appear as a hodgepodge of unconnected and contradictory ideas, another suggested. 'Ah!' Danish exclaimed: '*this* is precisely the point. The fragmentary nature of the *ghazal* demands utmost poetic concentration and restraint. The poet must say whatever he wants to say in two lines. Thus a *shair* is a highly condensed form of thought with multiple layers of meaning—and a good *shair* works on all levels. It also becomes an epigram, an instrument of thought and learning. Once you really understand a *shair*, you intuitively know all there is to know about metaphors and symbolism.'

By now the room had become really cold. Blankets were brought and distributed. Ehsan Danish continued:

The success of a *ghazal* depends not just on its use of imagery and metaphors, but also on its brevity and use of suggestive language. Once again the conventions of Urdu verse come to our aid. All *ghazals*, indeed each *shair*, revolves around a triangle: the lover, the beloved, and the obstacle or the rival. While there are countless variations to this triangle, the imagery involved is based on a convention. If you know the convention, you can unravel the symbolism and appreciate the depth of a verse. Thus the lover could be the *dil* (heart), *jazbah* (emotion), *parinda* (bird), *nazar* (gaze) or even Majnun (the doomed lover of classical romance); the beloved could be *husn* (beauty), *vijdaan* (intuition), *faza* (open space), *rukh* (face or direction) or Leila (the classical heroine) herself. And the obstacle could be *vahm* (dout), *aql* (reason), *saiyyad* (hunter), *niqab* (veil) or *duniya* (world). Now a *shair* containing these words and images could obviously have a surface erotic meaning; but it is what lies underneath this surface, the metaphysical, spiritual, mystical, philosophical or humanistic depth that is the true essence of a *ghazal*. Since even an ordinary peasant is well aware of this convention, the task of unraveling a *ghazal* is not beyond anyone. That is why Urdu verse is totally accessible and touches the soul of everyone.

A number of questions were raised. Are the conventions not restrictive? Do they not enchain artistic freedom? 'All forms of thought become civilised when bound by convention', Danish said:

The art of Urdu verse begins by mastering the convention and then transcending it. The imagery of the Urdu *ghazal* was originally developed for love poetry. Classical poets like Ghalib (d.1869) and his contemporaries infused the same imagery with philosophical, metaphysical and mystical dimensions. Iqbal (d.1938), Hasrat (d.1951) and other poets of the independence movement developed the imagery further by giving it a social and political expression. And now Faiz has transformed it yet again and brought in socialistic and nationalist themes. In Iqbal we see glimpses of Ghalib. In Faiz, we note the influence of Ghalib and Iqbal. The tradition continues but is itself transformed, broadened, enhanced. These are our greatest poets; they testify to the dynamic nature of the tradition of Urdu verse.

Danish adjusted his blanket and continued:

The poet transforms the imagery, adds a new layer of meaning, but he does something else. He brings his own notion of sound and resonance to his poetry. Read Ghalib and Mir Taqi Mir (1810) and see how different they sound. The use of certain sounds, its frequency, its peculiarity, reflect a poet's creative personality. Mir's despondent and contemplative moods cannot be conveyed by the sounds used by Ghalib for his non-conformist, rebellious attitude. Similarly, Iqbal's insistence that we shape our own destiny, his verve, his quest for the elevation of humanity towards a higher realm, call for a sound structure packed with power that could convey the urgency and intensity of his message. Iqbal's poetry thus has its own majestic vibrancy and grandeur. The particular use of sound, as well as the deeper content of his verse, gives a unique signature to a poet's writing. This is why you can stop a peasant in rural Punjab, recite a few verses and he will tell you whose verses you are reciting.

A poet lives what he writes, Danish said. When understanding reaches a certain point, it has no need for life. Live the poems of our great poets and see the point beyond which nothing more can be said.

On the stage of the Embassy *mushaira*, the animated conversation between Mahir al-Qadri and Hafeez Jallundhri had now reached a turning point. The second round of the recital began with Waheeda Naseem and followed the same order as the first. This time each poet started with requests and proceeded to recite more esoteric verses. The audience had long ceased to be mere onlookers; their reactions, the sway, sound and empathic power of their presence made them participants, as they reacted with ever more verve. The more enthusiastic individuals repeated the verses as though savouring each individual word and then excitedly shouted '*Muquerer, muquerer!*' (encore, encore). The poet repeated the same verse, new meanings were discovered, and furthers chants of '*Muquerer, muquerer!*' followed.

When Hafeez Jalandhri was invited to take the stage, he began by telling the audience that he had just composed a new poem which he would like to recite. 'Even in paradise' he began,

Even in paradise I am tormented
Even here my neighbour is a Mullah!

The crowd burst into laughter. Mahir could not take this sitting down. He got up and walked slowly to the front of the stage. 'Hafeez Shahib,' he said, 'surely you have gone to the wrong place. *This* place is not within your reach.' They roared with laughter and chanted '*Muquerer, muquerer!*' Mahir al-Qadri walked back slowly to where he was sitting, but he did not so much sit as lie down. Hafeez repeated his *shair*, and, in a mocking gesture, turned round and pointed at Mahir al-Qudri.

Hafeez Jalandhri was followed by Ehsan Danish who began with a powerful *ghazal* on the theme of death. As he recited,

There are no tragedies when there are no people
Under a blanket of earth, I too will sleep one day

Everything fell silent; nothing could be heard across the Embassy compound. No '*wah*', *wah*', no '*muquerer*', '*muquerer*'; just awe-inspiring, pregnant silence. And then the throbbing, gentle, unmistakable sobbing of Mahir al-Qadri. Danish continued, and a few verses later concluded the poem:

Don't forget the empty frames on the grave-stones
Who knows when, which photograph they will support

A clear, distinctive, loud 'Ahh' emanated from Mahir al-Qadri. According to the people sitting next to him, he was visibly shaken, sobbing uncontrollably. Then he fell silent. Pandemonium broke out as sections of the audience realised what had happened. It transpired that about a third of the audience consisted of doctors and surgeons all of whom ran towards the stage and simultaneously tried to examine Mahir Qadri. 'There is no pulse,' one murmured. 'No heartbeat either,' said another. 'Is the Maulana upset?' asked Hafeez Jalandhri. 'Surely he hasn't taken my *shair* to heart?' The Maulana Mahir had taken a *shair* to heart—but it wasn't that of Hafeez Jalandhri.

By the time the day had drawn to a close, Mahir al-Qadri was sleeping under a blanket of earth. Someone had placed a photograph, taken during the *mushaira*, on his tombstone.

A PERSON OF PAKISTANI ORIGINS

II

A poet also dies in *In Custody*, the Merchant Ivory film of the elegant and thoughtful novel by Anita Desai. Given that Desai co-wrote the screenplay, it is not surprising the film is faithful to the novel. The narrative itself is rather simple: a college lecturer, Deven, is sent by the editor of a literary magazine to interview the aging poet Nur Shahjehanabadi. The subject is Urdu poetry, but, this being an Ismael Merchant film, our scene has shifted. We are now in India, and that means much remains the same while everything has changed.

The opening sequence, before the credits, establishes Nur as a great poet: lying on his bed, Nur is composing a poem that we also hear on the soundtrack:

> *My mind is groping for a word*
> *A word as sweet as seduction and bitter as poison*
> *A word that bewitches but is full of rage*
> *My mind is groping for a word*
> *A word as brimming with passion as a gaze between two lovers*
> *As soft as a kiss*
> *A word shining like a sea of gold...*

But Nur is not just a great poet; he is in fact the last of the great Urdu poets. There is a ring of truth to this, given that the poetry he is writing and reciting is actually by Faiz Ahmad Faiz (d.1984), regarded as the last great Urdu poet of the twentieth century. A strong believer in freedom of expression, Faiz worked as a journalist and subscribed to socialism. Awarded the Lenin International Peace Prize in 1962, he spent several years in and out of jail on political charges. While some of his poems are simple and direct, many require knowledge of literary idiom to appreciate. In the film they are used to brilliant effect.

Nur lives in isolation with his two squabbling wives, drinks and eats too much, and is convinced that the great tradition of

Urdu poetry is gasping its last breaths. His house in Bhopal, a shabby, decaying *haveli* (mansion), serves as a metaphor for the Urdu language itself. Deven's assignment is to record Nur's poetic legacy and preserve it for posterity. When Deven first encounters Nur, the following exchanges take place:

> Deven: Murad Beg has sent this letter. He's the editor of *The Voice*.... He wants me to interview you. I'd be honoured if you would agree.

> Nur: Urdu poetry! If Urdu is no more, what significance has Urdu poetry? It's dead. Finished. Now you see its corpse. Lying here, waiting to be disposed of...

> Deven: Sir, we'll never allow that. Thousands read Murad's journal. Urdu textbooks are printed for schools. Even Mirpur college has an Urdu department.

> Nur: Do you teach there? Is that the department you teach in?

> Deven: No, the Hindi department. I have an MA in Hindi.

> Nur: Wonderful! You're a devotee of Urdu, but you teach Hindi. Why, young man?

> Deven: Sir, I teach to support my wife and child. I am a devotee of Urdu poetry. My desire ... is to serve Urdu in any small way.

Urdu and Hindi have an intimate relationship. Like everything else about the Raj-ified partitioned subcontinent from which both originate, their relationship is vexed and vexatious; like a set of rapids on a great river their history and interconnections are perilous to negotiate and threaten to overpower and swallow the cautious explorer. And having been Raj-ified, both are used to the processes of appropriation, misappropriation and purposeful obfuscation. Therefore it should be no surprise that the origins of Urdu are the subject of much dispute, myth making and academic dissension. What can be said is that Urdu emerged in the late twelfth and thirteenth century, when Muslims established themselves in northern India. The language of learning in India was Sanskrit, an ancient tongue which, rather like Latin, had ceased to be a living spoken language, though it was the root of many derivative dialects. The most common dialect used widely in and around Delhi, was known as *Khari Boli*, or standard speech. Members of the Muslim armies spoke Persian, Arabic and, to some extent, Turkish. Soon a large number of words from these languages were introduced into *Khari Boli*. The Muslim army stationed in Delhi from 1193 onwards was called *Urdu*, the Turkish word for army, or *Urdu e Mulla*, the Exalted Army. The language the army used to converse with the locals, an amalgam of *Khari Boli*, Persian, Arabic and Turkish, came to be known as Zaban-e-Urdu-e-Mulla—the Language of the Exalted Army. Which was eventually reduced simply to: *Urdu*. So an appropriately partitioned explanation runs: while Urdu is Persianised *Khari Boli*, Hindi is Sanskrit *Khari Boli*. What such arguments neatly elide is that language morphs and develops, it evolves slowly from its root to its tip. The root of Urdu, like Hindi, is Sanskrit. Basically, there is hardly any difference between the spoken languages. Loan words have been incorporated into both. The main difference comes in the written form: Urdu is written right to left in Persian/Arabic script, Hindi is written left to right in Devanagari script. Those who speak Urdu have no problem in understanding Hindi, and vice versa.

In Custody alludes to how Urdu has declined, indeed been suppressed, in India. A language of beauty and great literature is now mistrusted and despised in the land of its birth. Urdu is seen, particularly by nationalist Hindus, not just as the language of Muslims but as a Muslim language. There are no Urdu medium schools in the cities associated with the giants of Urdu literature—Delhi, Lucknow, Hyderabad. In Uttar Pradesh, where my Urdu-speaking grandparents lived and my parents were born, there is not a single Urdu medium primary or junior high school.

Not surprisingly, not many in India today can read or write Urdu. Indeed, even notable individuals who ought to know better, find it difficult to speak Urdu. Nur is played by Shashi Kapoor, the slender, perky actor of numerous Bollywood films I saw during my adolescence. In *In Custody*, Shashi Kapoor is anything but slender: grossly overweight, he plays Nur, as one critic pointed out, as 'a present day Balzac: fierce and wise yet with all the signs of having lived a little too well.' Nur's crumbling physical state is a metaphor for the state of Urdu poetry itself.

Setting the film in Bhopal is also a nod to the decline and decay of Urdu culture in India. The city where my father was born is renowned for its Urdu culture as well as its Mughul architecture. It was also the site of the devastating Union Carbide gas explosion in 1984. It was, as well, one of the cities hardest hit by violence and arson after the destruction of the Ayodhya mosque by Hindu extremists in 1992. Deven's journey to Nur's house through the narrow mucky streets of Bhopal, side-stepping domestic animals, puddles and everyday rubbish, serves as yet another metaphor for a decaying culture polluted beyond cleansing.

While Deven's first love is Urdu poetry, it is also a means of escape. He is frustrated by his life, a frustration he expresses by snapping at his wife, but perhaps he is disturbed by India as well. At the College, he has to put up with the crude and threatening behaviour of his superiors. He knows he and his interests are marginal to the dominant course of Indian development. For his project, his superiors can provide only an old-fashioned clapped-out tape recorder to record his interview. Those who surround Nur, the friends, admirers and hangers on, only pretend to love Urdu poetry. Not surprisingly, Deven is appalled by them. They are there for the freebees—the biryani, the whiskey, and the merry-making.

In contrast, Imtiaz Begum, the second and younger wife of Nur, 'junior *begum*', not only loves poetry, but writes, and wants to be seen as a poet. She is jealous of her husband: while he is

hailed as a great poet, she is ignored, indeed, not even considered
a poet. We see her at a recital where she is reciting *her* verse:

> *O desire of my heart*
> *If I so wanted*
> *All things would appear before me*
> *For the sake of my goal*
> *I will walk two miles*
> *And suddenly my goal*
> *will appear before me…*

On the basis of this *ghazal*, she is definitely a poet. The poem
used in the film is by Bhezad Lakhnavi, who, as the name suggests, was born in Lucknow in 1895, and started writing poetry
at the age of nine. After working for the Railways in India, he
moved to Pakistan to become a leading light of Radio Pakistan,
Karachi. Imtiaz Begum then proceeds to 'change the mood with
my new *ghazal*'.

> *O candle for the sake of the moth*
> *O candle for the sake of the moth*
> *Do me a little favour*
> *Flare up just once and then die*
> *When the master of this gathering appears*
> *O obsession of my heart,*
> *have it your way:*
> *I'll come to that gathering*
> *Just let me know when it's in full swing…*

Deven recognises it as Nur's writing. 'It's your poem. People
will think that it's hers,' he tells Nur.

In general, it is not easy to plagiarise the work of an established poet. Each poet has, or should have, a distinctive style
that is uniquely his or hers. But Urdu poetry has a particular
device to guard against theft. It is called *takhallus*: the name
under which a poet writes. This pen name is often introduced in

the last line of the *ghazal*, a seal that intrinsically binds the poem and the poet together. Urdu poets are generally known by their *takhallus*, which is sometimes a part of the poet's personal name (such as Mir Taqi Mir or Faiz Ahmed Faiz). Clearly, the Nur poem that Imtiaz Begum presented as her own did not have an embedded *takhallus*.

An angry Deven confronts Imtiaz Begum:

Imtiaz Begum: You think I'm a dancing girl. Perhaps that's what these men have told you. I'm a POETESS.

Deven: Poetess? You? You recited his poetry as your own. But I know it was Nur Sahib's verse.

Imtiaz Begum: We are both poets. An exchange of ideas is inevitable. What's wrong if a hint of his style is in my work? Hasn't he borrowed from the master?

Deven: Nur Sahib's unique poetry has an easily discernible style.

Imtiaz Begum: And all my couplets seem like his? You can't accept that a woman can write poetry.

Deven: Nur Sahib's stamp is on each of his lines. There is none like him.

Imtiaz Begum: Especially a woman, me in particular. You think a woman can be a dancing, singing courtesan but not a reflective being who expresses herself in her poems.

Why not? True. I've had no formal education nor a literary upbringing...but I have learned, even from Nur Sahib. I can write just as he can write.

Deven: Forgive me, but you cannot write like him, or be compared with him.

Imtiaz Begum challenges Deven to record her poems to see who is right. She gives Deven an anthology of her poetry: 'I'll show that poetry is not the preserve of men. You'll have to acknowledge that I'm a poetess. I'm a POETESS.' Indeed, she is a poet, but not of the calibre of Nur. So she steals his verse and presents it as her own. Her defence, and Deven's off-handed dismissal, reveal more about the position of women in Indian and Pakistani society than the quality of her poetry.

Poetic rivalries, such as the real one between Mahir al-Qadri and Hafeez Jallundhri, and the fictional one between Imtiaz Begum and Nur, are an integral part of the history of Urdu poetry. Every age, it is said, has a pair of Urdu poets who have a poetic brawl with each other. One is seen as a natural poet who writes from the heart and often gets most of the limelight. The other a master of language with the ability for stunning wordplay. The most famous example of this rivalry is that between Mir Taqi Mir (d.1810) and Sauda (d.1780). They could not be more different as poets; the only thing the two had in common is that they both lived in Delhi. Both are seen as great poets but Mir, the natural poet, is more famous; indeed, he is seen by some as *the* greatest Urdu poet. Sauda was among the first to write odes and satirise. He was a rowdy, cheerful person, quite contented with his comfortable life, who wrote with verve and grandeur. Mir, on the other hand, was poor, resentful, sad and disappointed in love. He wrote in simple, elegant, practically conversational language; there is brazen eroticism to some of his verses. While Mir recognised Sauda as a poet of equal stature, he was not too kind to his contemporaries. In one of his odes, he portrays himself as a gigantic serpent gulping down other poets, who are seen as rats, scorpions and snakes!

But the rivalry of Mir and Sauda was nothing compared to that of Mushafi (d.1824) and Insha (d.1817). Mushafi, a writer of great fluency, was the natural poet. A voracious reader, he could write in a number of styles, including those of Mir and Sauda, but had his own distinctive style that combined multiple influences. He moved from city to city, selling his poetry and seeking patronage from Nawabs. Insha was a jolly figure who spoke several languages and composed in Urdu, Persian, Arabic, Turkish and Punjabi. His poetry is full of humour and vivacity, reflecting much of his own life, which he spent demonstrating his skill and wit at royal courts in Delhi and Lucknow. He is said to have written the first book of Urdu grammar and rhetoric. Mushafi and Insha developed an intense rivalry which, with the passage of time, turned into open poetic warfare. Both abused each other with unsavoury language, often egged on by their admirers and patrons. Other noted rivalries include the quarrels between Atish (d.1846) and Nasikh (1838), Ghalib (1869) and Zauq (d.1854), and Dag (d.1905) and Amir (d.1900).

In Custody subtly nods not just at poetic rivalries but also at various aspects of the history of Urdu poetry. Deven's own blundering attempts to preserve the work of Nur prove futile. The recordings he makes turn out to be useless. Then Deven receives a parcel from Nur containing a collection of new verses on death, including his own imminent death: 'I leave them in your custody'. Finally, Deven has something to preserve and pass on to the future generations.

Perhaps. *In Custody* suggests that blind and unconditional lovers of modernisation, both in India and Pakistan, see little value in maintaining the legacy and tradition of Urdu poetry. Overjoyed at being the custodian of Nur's poetry, Deven rushes to tell the news to Siddiqui, his supporter and fellow tutor at the college. He arrives to see the Siddiqui *haveli* being demolished. 'So you've come to see my ancestral home vanish into the dust of Mirpur?' Siddiqui explains: 'A Delhi businessman has bought it. He'll build flats, with shops on the ground floor. There's to be a cinema at the back, with offices above.' Siddiqui is not interested in what Deven has to say: 'I've brought good news. Nur Sahib has left his new verse in my custody. I am now its executor.' Siddiqui retorts: 'I've got rid of my inheritance. I'm free.'

The last scenes of the film intercut the demolition of the Siddiqui *haveli*, a symbol of the genocide of a culture, with the funeral procession of Nur, to the accompaniment of one of the most powerful *ghazals* of Faiz/Nur:

> *Walk through this bazaar with feet in chains.*
> *Tears of rage are not enough*
> *Secret love is not enough.*
> *Walk through the bazaar today with feet in chains.*
> *With arms flung out in a dance of ecstasy*
> *With ashes on your head and a bloodstained cloak.*
> *Walk through the city of lovers.*
> *Walk through the bazaar today with feet in chains.*
> *Walk past the gaping crowds of the great and the small.*
> *Past the slings and arrows of slander.*
> *Past the unhappy dawn and the oppressed day.*
> *Walk through the bazaar today with feet in chains.*
> *In whom can they confide but me?*
> *I alone know who is sincere among lovers*
> *And who deserves to die.*
> *Prepare yourselves, all of you with aching hearts.*
> *Come, friends, let us go again towards our death.*

III

Somewhere in *In Custody*, Nur asks a significant question. 'You, who come from the land of Urdu: tell me, is Urdu still alive?'

It is, of course, a complex question that can be answered in a number of ways. One can say, for example, that Urdu will always live as long as there are Urdu-speakers. How many actually speak Urdu depends on how one defines Urdu. If Urdu is only spoken in Pakistan, then there are around 200 million Urdu speakers, a figure set to double within the next two decades. If one includes Urdu-speakers in India and Bangladesh, then the number could easily hit a billion: one-seventh of humanity. In which case Urdu will be around for some time. It's not the numbers, however, that will make the difference: it's the mindset, the understanding, the openness, the largeness of soul that matters. Or, to put it another way, the real question is an attitude to history and how that influences the present and will shape the future.

The message of *In Custody*, both the novel and the film, is that Urdu is dying in India. Or, more appropriately, being *killed* in India. Apart from three or four states, such as Maharashtra, Bihar and Uttar Pradesh, Urdu literacy is conspicuous in India largely by its absence. You can only study Urdu in half a dozen universities. And Urdu has been sponged from its most versatile vehicle: Bollywood films. I always thought that these films were in Urdu and the actors spoke Urdu. But in an NFT/Guardian interview with film critic Derek Malcolm, after the premier of *In Custody*, Shashi Kapoor categorically stated: 'I do not know how to speak Urdu. I had a special coach to teach me. It was very hard work. I am not going through that again.' It is an astounding declaration, one I find hard to comprehend. More than anything else, it sums up the state of Urdu in India for me.

Here I find myself, grudgingly, forced to acknowledge an entire thesis that usually makes me explode in revolt. Yes, I am brought kicking and screaming to the Indus Valley civilisation ploy. What is it that makes the history of the subcontinent? What occasions the land of Al-Hind? Answer: The Indus River along the course of which are found the earliest evidences of Indian civilisation at Mohenjodaro, Harrappa and Taxila—all of which are located in what is now Pakistan. What makes the history of Pakistani society and culture? You guessed it—much of it is located in what is now India. Partitioning history, like partitioning language and land area falsifies history and distorts imagination. History is subcontinental, interwoven, inclusive, compound and complex. Seeking to confine it to bifurcated entities invented at the behest of the hasty retreat of a hand-washing, no longer my responsibility colonial power is a *reductio ad absurdum* that damages the sense and reason of the two new nations

193

that came into being in 1947. The mutual denial, mutual rivalry, mutual disdain of both countries makes history a pick and mix of ramshackle shreds and patches from which self-serving myths emerge to service political and ideological purposes, but not the greater self-awareness or understanding of anyone.

What would India lose by losing Urdu? Urdu is a language of synthesis. That is another reason why it will continue to live. It is an amalgam of Persian, Arabic, Turkish, Sanskrit, and Hindi, and incorporates the conceptual outlook and modes of being and knowing of these cultures. To kill Urdu, you have to kill all its constituent parts. Urdu, not unlike some other languages, has a complex ecology which can change, mutate, transform like a living organism. All of this also makes Urdu, a language of metaphor and symbolism, intrinsically pluralistic. By losing Urdu, India is losing a major force for pluralism in society, something that is quite evident to me. Urdu poetry also serves both as a repository for, and the adhesive that preserves cultural and civilisational memory that is rapidly seeping away in India.

There is yet another point to consider. Urdu poetry was not just patronised by courts and courtiers, but also by common people—educated or not—Sufis and saints, humanists and champions of social justice. It exposes the reflective, contemplative and transcendental mind of the South Asian people. It refuses to succumb to dogma of any type—religious or secular. It inculcates humanism inspired by the spiritual worldview of syncretic India. Read Mir, Sauda (d.1781), Dard (d.1785), Astish (d.1846), Ghalib, Zauq (d.1854) and Iqbal to see what I mean. Without fail, it stands up to oppression of all varieties. Notice how much of classical Urdu poetry describes the suffering of South Asian people under the British Raj, as well as incites the oppressed to stand up to colonial rule. Consider, for example, the verses by Raja Ram Narain Mauzun, composed after the 1747 Battle of Plassey and the death of Nawab Sirajud Daula:

LOVE, DEATH AND URDU POETRY

O gazelle, you are witness to the death of Majnoon,
The mad (patriot) is no more, what now will be
the fate of the desert (country ruined by alien rule).

Or the famous short four-line poem, *qatah*, of Ghalib:

Surely today every English soldier considers himself God.
Everyone going from his house to the bazaar is struck with panic.
The market place looks like a slaughterhouse,
And the houses look like prisons.
As if every particle of dust in Delhi
thirst for the blood for the Muslims.

Or Iqbal's poem on the massacre of 1919 the Jalianwala Bagh in Amritsar:

To every visitor, the dust-particle of this garden declares:
Beware of the treachery of the times
The seed (of freedom) here was sown with martyrs blood
Which you must now nurture with your tears.

Urdu poetry has not just preserved the history and memory, shaped not just pluralism and humanism, but also moulded the imagination of India. Without Urdu poetry, India has no imagination worthy of attention.

In Pakistan, needless to say, it is a somewhat different story. As a 'national' language Urdu is taught from kindergarten to the university. But Urdu poetry is also in decline in Pakistan. The *mushairas* are not as common as they were during my infant days in Bahawalnagar and Montgomery (now Sahiwal). The frequent poetry recitals on radio and television have been replaced with shouting matches, ironically called 'Talk Shows'. The art and literature coverage of numerous television channels is abysmal. The masses are fed a constant diet of 'breaking news', trivia and sensational diatribe. The poet as national icon has been replaced with pop stars as national celebrities.

After Josh, there is no one to capture the anger and the restlessness of the masses. After Faiz, there is no humane voice to agitate for social change and reform. After Ehsan Danish, there is no one who has suffered and is thus deeply touched by the suffering of others. Not surprisingly, Pakistan too is losing its tradition of pluralism and humanism, along with its cultural memory.

In *In Custody*, Nur tells a fellow poet: 'You recite verses like lullabies. You need power and resonance. A cannon roar.' It is the cannon roar that has gone from Urdu poetry in Pakistan.

The roar is all too evident in the poem by Faiz, '*Aaj bazaar amin*' ('Today in the Bazaar'), used in the final funeral procession scenes of *In Custody*. It is full of references to secret love and the city of the beloved, and can be read as a potent love poem. But it can also be read as a clarion call to dissent. Dance, the poet urges us, in the bazaar, a place without walls and ceiling, with your shackles and blood-soaked garbs, in an ecstasy of freedom. Do not suffer in silence, he tells the oppressed, the downtrodden, the marginalised; stand up to oppression, exploitation and the injustices of rulers and feudal landlords, the restrictions of social order, the suffocation of fossilised tradition, the bigotry of religious orthodoxy and the alienation of modernity and secularism. But be aware of the cost. Those who speak truth to power face the 'arrow of false charge, stone of accusation'; they are ridiculed, falsified, subjugated. The truth may not prevail; the day of the dance may be followed by the 'morning of sorrow, day of failure', the time of anguish and torture. But the grief and sorrow should not dissuade us from our continuous struggle for justice. A cause in which the poet himself is willing to sacrifice his own life: 'Let me go to be executed.'

IV

In the early 1970s, while I was still an undergraduate student, I attended a *mushaira* at the Pakistani High Commission in London. I don't remember much about that *mushaira* except that one particular poet caused a great deal of excitement: ibn-e-Insha (1927–1978). Apart from being a poet, he was a well-known humourist, travel writer, columnist and a diplomat. His poetry regularly appeared in literary magazines and newspapers. My father described his poetry as a combination of classical and modern, influenced by Mir, with an accent on the grief and despair prompted by modernity. He recited a new poem: '*Insha ji utto, ab kuch karo*' (Insha get up, it's time to leave). It is about a despondent man, the poet himself, who, after spending a night at an unsavoury gathering, suddenly decides to move on. He returns to his house before dawn and tries to think of a suitable excuse for his beloved. He thinks his existence is meaningless and, disenchanted with the city itself, he decides to migrate. I liked the poem, but at that time thought it was about a man disenchanted both with love and life.

Then, a few years later, I heard the poem again. This time it was in the voice of the celebrated Pakistani *ghazal* singer, Amanat Ali Khan. I was mesmerised. Amanat had transformed himself into the protagonist of the poem. Now I saw it not as a love poem, but a commanding indictment of the alienation of urban life, the meaningless existence endangered by modernity. Reflect, observe: the metropolis has no space or place for the *jogi* and those who seek inner calm.

Amanat Ali Khan first performed the *ghazal* on Pakistani Television (PTV) in January 1974. He died suddenly, age fifty-two, in September of that year. A few months later, it is said, his producer, Khalil Ahmad, also died. Ibn-e-Insha himself died four years later in January 1978. He was fifty-one. Amanat Ali came from a noted family of *ghazal* singers. His son, Asad Amanat Ali, was also a famous singer of classical *ghazals*. In a concert for PTV in 2006, Asad sang a number of *ghazals* as well as popular film songs. He ended the concert by preforming '*Insha ji utto*'. It turned out to be his last concert; '*Insha ji utto*' the last *ghazal* he sang. He died a few months later in April 2007, age fifty-two.

Is there a connection between the poem and the four deaths? It is reported that Ibn-e-Insha himself thought that the *ghazal* was cursed. Soon after he wrote the poem, he contracted Hodgkin's disease. *Ghazal* singers are not renowned for good health. Maybe the death of Amanat and Asad has more to do with their physical constitution than the poem. But there is an aura of death surrounding the *ghazal*. Despite its popularity, *ghazal* singers have stayed away from the poem. No one has sung the *ghazal* since Asad Amanat Ali's concert. Perhaps they are just superstitious. It is, after all, *only* a poem. Nevertheless, I wonder: once is an incident, twice a coincidence, but a third and a fourth time? Is there a pattern? I don't know. I will let you decide. All I know is that Urdu poetry should be like genuine history: alive, open-ended, always throwing up new and challenging questions.

6.

....

MY VANISHING UNCLE

....

I

My Uncle Waheed was a superhero. His superpower was the ability to disappear in the blink of an eye. One minute he is here, standing next to you, the next he has gone. We called him Waheed Mammu—*mammu* being Uncle in Urdu. But *mammu* is a particular type of Uncle: the brother of your mother. The younger brother of one's father is called *chacha*; the elder brother is *tayya*. Waheed Mammu was one among my four *mammus*. The eldest was Fareed Mammu, who, after spending a short spell in the navy, became a civil servant. He had eight children and suffered, most of his life, from arthritis and severe pain in his joints. Then came Rasheed Mammu, a lawyer who worked in Saudi Arabia for a few years. Waheed Mammu was next, followed by Shahid Mammu. As long ago and far away as I can remember, all the *mammus* lived together, or very near each other, in Karachi. Out of respect, I never referred to their wives, our aunties, by their real names. Instead, nicknames were the norm. So Fareed Mammu's wife was known as *bathrine mummani*—the best possible aunt! Rashid Mammu's wife was *choti mummani*—younger aunt. My maternal grandmother was *Nanni jaan*, and everyone, including the neighbours, called her that. My mother was universally known as Mumsey. I labour these points because, in the tangled web of a Pakistani extended family, it is important to get the nomenclature and nicknames right. Certain members of the family are only known by their nicknames. One has to look at their identity cards to discover their real names.

A PERSON OF PAKISTANI ORIGINS

Waheed Mammu was always special. But people saw him more as a funny—both peculiar and ha! ha!—person, somewhat unhinged. He was a short, slim man, with an unkempt, unruly, beard that flowed in all directions. As a child he suffered from a skin disease that left its mark on his face. Always in a white *kurta pajama*, on his head ever a thin cotton cap—a 'Jinnah cap', though sometimes he wore a black cap, reminiscent of a fez but without the long tassel of loosely hanging threads. He was born in Bhopal, India, in 1946, just over a year before Partition and the creation of Pakistan. After migrating to Pakistan with the entire family, he spent most of his childhood in Diplapur and Karachi. The family suffered severe economic hardship; the situation worsened for Waheed Mammu in particular after the loss of his father. He was brought up by and in the house of Farid Mammu, for whom he had high regard. He was the only person Waheed Mammu paid attention to, and feared a little, apart from his mother.

As a teenager, Waheed Mammu had a large, round, red nose, not unlike W.C. Fields of *My Little Chickadee* fame. W.C. Fields nose was a product of his incessant drinking; Waheed Mammu's nose was the outcome of a skin disease. That did not stop him from becoming a constant butt of jokes. The other children in the family used to call him 'Pakora nose'—after the popular South Asian deep-fried patty of onions, potato and spinach. I only called him 'Pakora nose' once, as a little boy while we still lived in Karachi. Waheed Mammu gave me one of his rare sombre looks—a look that stated plainly 'I don't expect *that* from you'. It was enough to chasten me and change my behaviour. This was one of his peculiarities. Waheed Mammu, always playful, could transform people with a single glance. He used his facial expressions as a potent weapon: his smile could melt a heart of stone; his frown could convert a wicked individual. When you looked at his face directly, you were mesmerised; for that moment you were his and he could mould and shape you in any way he desired.

Waheed Mammu dropped out of school when he failed his matriculation examination. He could read and write Urdu, but knew little else. As a young man, his favourite pastime was reading the biographies of Muslim Sufi saints. He would often read them aloud to other children. By the time he was in his late teens, he had acquired a reputation as a storyteller: children from the family and neighbourhood would surround him, and Waheed Mammu would give a performance, enacting the lives of great mystics with real gusto. Children loved him largely because he was so childlike himself: he had little concern for his personal well-being or for the material world that surrounded him. He was, and looked, exquisitely simple and innocent: lies, deception, back-biting, greed and jealousy were totally unknown to him. Initially, people thought that because he could not do anything else, he devoted most of his time to prayer: he frequently got up in the middle of the night to pray, he fasted often, read the Qur'an frequently. There is a long-established tradition in Pakistan: a person who has no skills and abilities, who is basically illiterate, ends up being the Imam of a mosque. So, people thought Waheed Mammu was destined to be a *mauluvi* of a neighbourhood mosque. Slowly, we all began to realise that Waheed Mammu had a special vocation; a strange mystical aura that surrounded his very being.

Now the story I have to tell stretches over many years. It accumulated episodically like my acquaintance with Pakistan after being uprooted and relocated to Britain. It is a tale with a continuing theme: my family, the anchor that kept bringing me back to the land of my birth to that belonging which is my origin. All the gaps and intermissions are not voids when it comes to family. There is the constant flow of news, gossip and vital family counsel that continues unabated despite time-distance or varying degrees of fashionable disinterest or fashionable interest. In the bunker of nuclear family in which we lived in London, swimming in the brimming ocean of family and family connections that was and is life in Pakistan seems an alternate reality—a parallel universe. All I can say is I exist there too. I am always there because my absence makes no difference to the relatives, and I am who they and I expect when I reappear in the midst of their warm embrace. Over the years, I have come to appreciate the levels and meanings of my own appearances and disappearances among them; those of Waheed Mammu are something quite distinct. He was a mystery of the ages the entire family had to resolve.

In the late seventies, when I first visited Karachi after migrating to Britain, I became quite close to Waheed Mammu. Whenever I went there I stayed at his overcrowded house. To do anything else would have been seen as a major insult. But there was another reason. My childhood in Pakistan was spent growing up with Gudu and Guda, the eldest sons of Fareed Mammu. To this day, I have difficulty remembering their real names, a point made to embarrassing effect on a recent visit. I and my serial co-author were in Pakistan to prepare a guest issue for a British magazine. A stop in Karachi was a necessary part of the exercise and no stop in Karachi was possible without a visit to Gudu. QED. Now my co-author has, over the years, listened to endless stories about Pakistan, and read everything I have written on the subject of my family there. She was more than familiar with the character Gudu. In the bustling forecourt of the arrival terminal of Karachi airport I was able to present with enthusiasm equivalent to drumroll and fanfare: '*This* IS Gudu!' She responded effusively: 'Oh my! Gudu! Gudu how are you? So good to finally meet you!' etc. I was surprised when the following day she sheepishly admitted that Gudu had complained, indeed had told her off for addressing him as Gudu in public and in front of his own children. Why would he say that I asked her? 'Excuse me you're the

Pakistani expert here,' she replied. I contemplated my feet a while to let the frisson pass. Of course, Gudu is a childish nickname and when we grow up we put away childish things (more's the pity I often think). But if not Gudu, what could I call my dearest cousin? One can hardly turn around at our time of life and ask—'so what actually is your name?' After a long pause co-author observed: 'Don't sweat it. We've just found out that my brother gave all four of his children family names without ever knowing it! I mean we had no idea his son David has the name of our estranged paternal grandfather. We always called him the Welsh shortform for grandfather, Guo. Well, you don't call grandfathers by their first name!' Cousins, I suspect, are a different matter. Maybe there is some coming of age ceremony where adult names are revealed, and I missed it. But I can never stop calling him Gudu, as I did when we played together. Spending time with him in Karachi was one way of rekindling and reliving my childhood memories of Pakistan.

I would join my cousins in teasing Waheed Mammu. 'Waheed Mammu,' we would say, 'you are our teacher and leader. Lead us wherever you want.' Then, we would have mock coronations to appoint him as our Guru. He would go along with the proceedings, playfully making his 'inaugural speech' in Urdu, save for the first introductory sentence in English: 'Thank you, please! I am gratefully honoured.'

Occasionally, the speech would be interrupted by the disruptive behaviour of one of the 'audience', triggering angry reproaches from the speaker. At times, the rally would descend to dogfights ending in my cousins and I seeking forgiveness by mockingly massaging him from head to toe.

During one hot summer night in 1977, we persuaded Waheed Mammu to give us a theological lecture. We were sitting upstairs in a small room inside the house, and outside, on the veranda, slept Farid Mammu on his *charpoy*, shaded by the papaya tree.

Waheed Mammu did not wish to wake his elder brother, who would undoubtedly scold him severely. So Waheed Mammu started to relate the entire story of Noah and the Great Flood in mime. It was a virtuoso performance, complete with all the theatrical expressions of an accomplished actor. The demands of reality-acting soon exhausted him; worse, he had to answer nature's very urgent call. The toilet lay beyond the impassable domain of Farid Mammu's *charpoy* on the veranda. With some effort, he was persuaded to leap over the wall into the courtyard of the neighbour's house to use his toilet. We three cavaliers banded together to pick him up and with all our might hurl him over the wall. Our stratagem lacked somewhat in physical prowess. After a number of attempts, Waheed Mammu eventually managed to flop rather than leap and drop over to the other side of the wall—not on the expected patch of greenery but onto the neighbour himself, who at that exact moment was fully engaged in the very physiological function of Waheed Mammu's desire!

That Waheed Mammu had the propensity to disappear was first brought to the family's attention by his mother, Nani Jaan. Waheed Mammu had a special relationship with Nani Jaan, who treated and pampered him as a baby. Occasionally, she would scold him, and every now and then, when she was totally exasperated, she would give him a clip around the head. He seemed to enjoy these demonstrative remonstrations. When he had displeased her, he would stand in front of her, head bowed down, waiting for a smack. She knew she couldn't change him, but that did not stop her trying. Two things in particular concerned her: job and marriage. She urged everyone to find him a job—but, of course, everyone knew that Waheed Mammu, who had by now acquired the appellation of *Maulana* (religious master or teacher) was not interested in finding a job and was not going to keep one if he actually found employment. Eventually, at Nani Jaan's instance, he was pushed into a job as 'electrical helper' at the

Powerhouse of the Military Engineering Service in Karachi. Nani Jaan would make sure that he went to work every morning, making different members of the family responsible for escorting him there. Reluctantly he would be marched to his factory, but slip away within a couple of hours, occasionally coming home to Nani Jaan to complain that the work was not interesting. He was equally disinterested in his salary. On those occasions when he was due wages, he never turned up to actually receive them. The episode came to an end after a year and a half. But Nani Jaan did not give up. A year or so later, she found him another job—this time as a helper at a government outlet distributing basic supplies. He seemed to like this job, and, by all accounts, worked hard. He would pick up any 'wasted' grain, sugar or rice, which would fall onto the floor during the course of work, and save it in a small bag to feed birds on his way back home. Eventually, the manager accused him of stealing and sacked him. After that, the file on Waheed Mammu's job prospects was closed with permanent effect.

The employment distraction removed, focus could now be shifted fully to his disappearing act. Why would he just take off in the middle of a conversation? How could he disappear from sight within moments? Where did he go? What did he do?

II

Waheed Mammu was a brisk walker. Within minutes of being dropped at his place of work, when employed at the Powerhouse, he would be treating himself to a snack a mile or two away at a road-side café-cum-baker's oven or praying in a local mosque. I thought his facility to move around so fast was based on his ability to make instant friends. He warmly greeted everyone he encountered; he hugged everyone, often complete strangers, when he met them. He could walk into any gathering and his unique style would instantaneously capture everyone's attention; he would then proceed to entertain and amuse the assembled crowd with his unique way of talking. Simply by looking at him one could discern that this man was different: he had no regard for social constraint, his priorities were very different, he lived a separate life and existed in a parallel universe. I was convinced it had to be this ability to establish an instant deep rapport that enabled Waheed Mammu to move about so rapidly and efficiently. This suspicion was confirmed when I found myself walking in the streets of Model Colony with Gudu and Waheed Mammu. We were chatting as we walked. One moment I half turned to look at Gudu, then a split second later turned again towards Waheed Mammu, to discover he had gone. We immediately instituted a 360 degree search only to observe him comfortably ensconced on the back seat of a motorbike, waving to us. Gudu pointed out that the driver of the bike, now casually pulling away, was a complete stranger. He clearly liked Waheed Mammu, I thought, to give him a lift. At that particular moment, I envied Waheed Mammu's ability to develop a seemingly deep and empathetic understanding with strangers so quickly.

On another occasion, the three of us were going to visit Zahida *khala*—my mother's younger sister. She lived very far from Model Colony in a remote area of Karachi called Maripur, a rather poor neighbourhood with three main characteristics. First, it is distinguished by the sheer diversity of its denizens: Sindhis, Punjabis, Kashmiris, Pathans, Gujaratis, Mohajirs (those who migrated from India); Sunni Muslims, Shia Muslims, Ismaili Muslims, Bora Muslims, Memons (community of Muslims from western part of India known for their business acumen) and Hindus—to mention a few of the known varieties. Second, Maripur is host to one of the largest air force bases in the country: Pakistan Air Force (PAF) Base Masroor, originally called PAF Maripur. Third, Maripur is practically impossible to get to from anywhere in Karachi. You have to go to the centre of the city, Saddar, to catch one of the two buses that will eventually deposit you in Maripur. When I say catch, I mean catch: buses in Karachi do not actually stop at bus stops. They just slow down. So you have to run and catch it while it is still moving. However, even if you manage to catch up to the bus, it may not be possible to get on. By a well-established law of nature, buses in Karachi are full to the brim, with passengers sometime hanging dangerously from the doors. So there was no way I was going to be persuaded to catch a bus to Maripur. Gudu recommended that we take a rickshaw.

A rickshaw is a unique Pakistani institution: basically it is a Vespa scooter transformed—by unlettered and untutored but highly skilled local engineering—into a three wheel contraption. The whole machine is shaped like a quarter-ellipsoid. You sit in the back behind the driver and hold on to the metal bar covered with thick plastic tape. For sheer speed and manoeuvrability, the motor rickshaw cannot be outmatched. It can go anywhere, however small the alley, however bad the road. Often the drivers forget their machines have two wheels in the back and try to negotiate openings in congested roads only big enough to take the front part of the rickshaw. A truly hair-raising experience is thus often had by the innocent passenger(s) sitting in the back. I say sitting, although it is not all that easy to actually *sit* in a rickshaw given the state of the roads in Karachi. Again, to describe them as roads is an act of generosity. Once the driver kick starts his machine, passengers touch the seat about every fifteen to twenty seconds. During rush hour—which lasts most of the day—a rickshaw may carry up to five people, excluding the driver: two standing in front on either side of him, three sitting in the back. The whole machine is designed and built in such a way that if it overturns, which it does more frequently than one would imagine, the passengers are not thrown out. I have seen quite spectacular crashes with passengers walking out shaken but unstirred and unscathed.

We walked out of Farid Mammu's house to look for a rick-shaw, which can be as difficult to find as it is to catch a bus. It was late afternoon, the sun was in a vengeful mood, and we were its main victims. The three of us were profusely drenched in sweat. We waited and waited; eventually with some relief Gudu spotted a vacant rickshaw. The three of us jumped in. 'Maripur, *yar*, Maripur,' Gudu said to the rickshaw wallah. 'Hurry up, let's move.' But the only sign of movement I could detect was on the face of rickshaw wallah. He was vigorously chewing a *paan* and chocolate coloured *paan* juice was dribbling from his lips. He took some time to swallow the paan, and then said calmly: 'Only two passengers, please!'

'What?' said Gudu, clearly agitated. 'Two, three, what differ-ence does it make?' Rickshaw wallah repeated himself. 'Only two passengers, please!'

Gudu pointed to a nearby rickshaw: 'Look at that rickshaw. It has five people in it.'

'In that case,' replied the rickshaw wallah, a bit irritated, 'you take that rickshaw. This one carries only two passengers.'

Gudu looked at me. I looked at Waheed Mammu. 'It's ok,' Waheed Mammu said. 'You two take the rickshaw. I will make my own way.' He jumped out and waved, as the rickshaw pulled away. 'See you there,' I shouted.

As the rickshaw meandered through the streets of Karachi, I noticed that the rickshaw-wallah was chewing more than a *paan*. He was, you might say, getting more *bhang* (Cannabis indica) for his buck and hence had to take utmost care that his physical transport did not follow the flight path his mind was on. No wonder he insisted on only two passengers: better to scrape up the remains of two people than three. There were a couple of moments when I thought we might be crushed by a lorry or hit by a bus, but somehow the rickshaw was manoeuvred through all such obstacles with consummate skill. We arrived at Zahida *khalas* house in good time.

Gudu knocked at the door. 'Zahida *khala*, Zahida *khala*. Look who has come to see you.' The door opened. Waheed Mammu stood beside the door with a grin on his face. I could hear Zahida *khala* shouting from her living room: 'Waheed, have you been to the bazaar to buy the milk. Have you made the tea?'

'Yes.' Waheed Mammu replied. 'Come down. The tea is ready.'

Gudu and I looked at each other in total amazement. It was not just that Waheed Mammu had managed to get to Zahida *khalas* place before us but he had already been to the bazaar to buy the milk and had made the tea!

'Waheed Mammu,' I could not contain myself. 'How on earth did you get here before us?'

'There is more than one way to travel,' he said, smiling.

We had to travel some distance during the winter of 1977. I was getting married. My wedding party, consisting of all my *mammu*s and *mumanni*s, *chacha*s and *chachi*s, *khala*s and a long string of cousins, was, *en masse*, going to make the journey of some hundreds of miles from Karachi to Bahawalnagar, where the wedding was to take place. The entire extended family had gathered at Fareed Mammu's house. Taxis, rickshaws and other modes of transport had been organised to take everyone to the railway station.

A day before our departure, Nani Jaan fell ill. She insisted that the wedding party should proceed as planned. She would stay in Karachi. But someone had to stay behind to look after her. No one volunteered. Nobody could be induced, bribed or cajoled to stay and look after Nani Jaan. Finally, by an overwhelming consensus, it was decided that Waheed Mammu was the ideal person for the job. It only remained for him to be persuaded. A plan was hatched.

Nani Jaan lived adjacent to Farid Mammu, in a small house. Always under construction, it had one large window-less room, which opened onto a veranda. Early on the day of departure, a group of my cousins grabbed Waheed Mammu when he was offering his morning prayers and locked him in the room. A *charpoy* was placed in front of the door: a bed for Nani Jaan. She slept on the *charpoy* with keys to the door under her pillow. 'Don't worry,' she told us. 'I will not let him out of the room till all of you are safely in Bahawalnagar.' Finding himself alone with Nani Jaan, we thought, Waheed Mammu would be forced to stay and look after her.

The wedding party made its way to the Karachi City Station. It is the oldest station in Pakistan—and it shows. It is a majestic, if dilapidated, building that had seen little improvement since the tracks were laid way back in the 1850s. We had made 'advance booking' and fought our way through the bulging crowd to the appropriate platform. Trains in Pakistan have names—some are named after famous personalities, some after famous places. For example, Bahauddin Zakariya Express, which goes from Karachi to Multan, is named after a famous Sufi saint who lived in Multan during the thirteenth century. Bolan Mail, the train that goes from Karachi to Peshawar, is named after the strategically located Bolan Pass, which has served as a gateway to South Asia. We were going to take Fareed Express, named after Baba Fareed Shakar Ganj, a twelfth-century Punjabi Sufi saint. The 'Express' in the name refers to the fact that it crawls from Karachi to Lahore, a distance of around 800 miles, taking over 27 hours to complete the journey. However, not all of the train that starts in Karachi ends up in Lahore: parts of the train spilt at various junctions and go to different parts of the country. To get to Bahawalnagar, we had to get into one specific coach, which splits from the main train at Samasata Junction, and heads for our destination. To identify the designated Bahawalnagar coach was not an easy task;

to get all the wedding party, complete with the luggage, into that coach was an even more complex undertaking.

We hired two station porters—commonly known as coolies. The plan was that one of them would go to the terminus where the train was being prepared, identify and get into the Bahawalnagar coach. The other one would stay with us. When the train arrived at the station, the two coolies would communicate with each other and work in conjunction to get the entire wedding party, plus mountains of luggage, into the right coach. The coolies assured us that they had extensive experience of performing these tasks, and there was nothing to worry about.

After several minutes, the train finally crept into the platform. The platform erupted with people. They engulfed the train. We looked eagerly for the coolie who was supposed to be in the designated Bahawalnagar coach but he was nowhere to be seen. There was panic on the face of the coolie who was with us as well as most of the men in the wedding party. Then suddenly we heard a familiar voice. To our astonishment, Waheed Mammu was leaning out of a window and shouting 'this way, this way'. 'This is the Bahawalnagar coach. This way.' The entire wedding party moved in unison towards Waheed Mammu. Through the door as well as a number of its windows, we pushed, jumped and climbed our way into the coach—followed by our luggage which was handled with equal disrespect. Waheed Mammu had secured a berth for me. I was picked up by a hardy cousin and dumped on the berth.

When most members of the wedding party had found a place to sit or, if they were lucky, lie down, all eyes turned towards Waheed Mammu. 'How did you get out of the locked room?'; 'How did you find the Bahawalnagar coach?'; 'Who is looking after Nani Jaan?' He faced a barrage of questions from the elderly as well as the young. Waheed Mammu gave no replies. The senior members of the family began to shout and scold him, but this was not a coherent scolding. It was more a long and meandering stream of abuse in several languages. But all Waheed Mammu said was 'there is nothing to worry about; she is in good hands.' He looked at me as though he was sharing a secret. 'There is more than one way to travel,' he said, before jumping off the train as it shrilly pulled away from the platform.

There are around twenty stops between Karachi and Samasata. Waheed Mammu reappeared at a number of stations—once with a tray of *barfi*, once with a basket of oranges. We spent the night in what seemed like a wilderness at Samasata Junction, after our coach split from the main train. Here Waheed Mammu appeared with a handful of blankets and received generous prayers from older members of the wedding party. During the entire week of the wedding celebrations he would appear, always at some crucial moment, and then, with equal regularity, disappear again.

III

Waheed Mammu's own marriage was both a source of concern as well as delight for all around him. Nani Jaan's fondest wish was to see him married. 'There must be some woman somewhere who will somehow marry my somewhat rascal of a son,' she would say. 'Has not God created everything in pairs? Somewhere in Pakistan is his other half. Perhaps she is just as much of a half-wit as he is. But she is *there*. All we need to do is to find her.' Numerous aunties, from the family, neighbourhood as well as remote corners of the country, were always on the lookout for a wife for Uncle Waheed. He enjoyed encouraging both his mother and others: 'Maybe a woman will change me,' he would say. 'But first she has to catch me!' A few women in the family enjoyed teasing Waheed Mammu; they would fabricate stories of proposals and then describe the potential wife in elaborate detail. They would encircle Waheed Mammu and start regaling him with the virtues of the woman they had found for him. He would play along with them. 'Tell me more,' he would say. 'How educated is she? What is her family like?' Eventually, the woman in question would turn out to be 70, bed-ridden or dead. Normally, Nani Jaan would put a halt to the proceedings before they got too rowdy. Occasionally, Waheed Mammu would take matters in his own hands—he would pretend to flog the gathering with his handkerchief instantaneously transformed into a whip. The women would realise that Waheed Mammu had had enough and quietly disperse.

Sometimes I detected a state of ecstasy on his face—but that was a sign of serious trouble to come. For when *Maulana*—in that state he really was someone to look up to—looked funnier than usual, he would totally lose himself. He would be discovered standing stark naked in the middle of the veranda, or wandering in his birthday suit, covered in dust, in the streets. Family members tell the story of the 1965 war between India and Pakistan. In those days, Waheed Mammu lived in Manora, an island near Karachi. During the first week of war, when air raids were expected, there was a complete blackout in Karachi. Everyone sat inside the house, all huddled together. At about midnight, there was a loud knock at the door. The whole family was scared out of their wits. When they managed to summon up enough courage to open the door, they discovered two dozen angry military officers, complete with machine guns, demanding to know what was happening. What was happening was Waheed Mammu—standing naked on the roof, in a state of ecstasy, under a full flowing tap, highlighted by full illumination with all lights on!

One day, during a visit to Karachi, I found Waheed Mammu standing in front of Nani Jaan, his head bowed in anticipation of a clip on the head. Nani Jaan was scolding him: it was a free-form scolding, full of anger and anguish, but also peppered with generous, yet mild, curses—'Why has God not provided you with wings so you could fly away from my sight?', 'Why is God pun-

ishing me for being a loving mother?' and, my favourite, 'If I was
not a virtuous woman I would understand why you behave like a
bastard.' I always thought that the Urdu word for bastard—
haram zadah—has a wonderful poetic ring to it. It sounds not so
much like an abuse but more like a lyrical ticking off. There was
a third person sitting on the *charpoy*.

'What has Waheed Mammu done?' I asked him.

'Mohatram,' (Respected Sir), the man said in his best Urdu,
'My name is Jagat Baba; I am a respected elder of this good
neighbourhood of ours. The shopkeepers and *thailay wallas* have
dispatched me as their representatives to lodge a complaint
against the Maulana.'

'What is your complaint?' I asked.

It turned out that Waheed Mammu had been sneaking in to
the neighbourhood mosques and making the call to prayer an
hour earlier than the schedule. The shopkeepers, more used to
keeping time though prayer than keeping a clock, had all made
an unscheduled visit to the mosque.

'And another thing,' Jagat Baba said, wagging his finger,
'Whenever your uncle leads the prayer, he habitually leaves the
congregation standing.'

'What do you mean?' I was puzzled.

'I mean while the congregation is bowing or prostrating he
walks off to relieve himself!'

I was still laughing when Jagat Baba left. Nani Jaan had
exhausted herself through cursing. I put my arms around her and
escorted her to the *charpoy*.

'I just do not understand my own son!' she muttered. 'What
am I going to do with him?'

'Waheed Mammu will be Waheed Mammu,' I replied. 'You
will just have to accept it. There is nothing anybody can do.'

'*That,*' she replied, in a matter of fact way, 'I do understand'.
She paused for a deep breath. 'But I just do not understand
where he disappears to.'

216

I kept quiet. Nani Jaan was in deep thought.

'Where does he go? One minute he is here, the next he has evaporated. How does he vanish?' She looked towards me to provide an answer.

I shook my head. Shrugged my shoulders. I placed my head on her shoulders and she started gently massaging my head with her right palm.

'My life is an open book,' she continued. 'The lives of my children and grandchildren are there for all to see. There is only one mystery in my life.' She paused again to take a deep breath. 'The mystery of *haram zadah* Waheed.'

She started to cry. 'I only desire one thing before I die.'

'To know,' I said, as she continued to massage my head, 'how Waheed Mammu performs his vanishing trick...'

'And where does he go when he vanishes,' she added.

There, at that moment, I resolved to unravel the enigma that was Waheed Mammu.

IV

I decided to appoint two young members of the family to constantly follow Waheed Mammu. 'Stay with him wherever he goes,' they were instructed. But he proved too fast and too foxy for them. After over two years of effort they turned up little information. During one visit to Karachi in early 1980s, a plan was hatched to slow Waheed Mammu down just a little bit— enough so he could be followed more effectively. He liked both to give and receive a massage; indeed, at any given time, someone in our family was giving or receiving a massage. The elder women of the house were constantly being chased by their grandchildren to 'press their legs'. Whenever I saw Fareed Mammu he was spread-eagled on his *charpoy* on the veranda, with a young person on top of him skilfully using his feet to relieve the aches and pains of an aging body. We decided to give Waheed Mammu a massage. So, a professional masseur, a huge muscular man who was a part-time wrestler, was hired to attend to Waheed Mammu. He was given strict instructions to show no mercy. One day, when Waheed Mammu arrived on his usual whirlwind visit to the house, the wrestler grabbed him, pinned him down to a *charpoy*, and proceeded to give him a rigorous massage. To begin with, Waheed Mammu struggled—but then he began to enjoy the experience. Soon, the wrestler was rubbing all kinds of oils on his body. When the wrestler finished his task, Waheed Mammu took his time to get up. When he did get up, he walked in an uncoordinated way, as though he was slightly disorientated. He did a random walk on the veranda and then left—proceeded by his two trusted followers.

Our plan worked. For the next few days Waheed Mammu moved not with his usual speed and manoeuvrability, but leisurely and a little uncomfortably. The rigorous pleasures of the massage gave way to pains in the joints and the special oil made him feel somewhat heavy and sluggish. The boys could follow him relatively easily. They discovered that Waheed Mammu was linked to a mystical group and had a number of followers of his own, who venerated him as a mystic. People from neighbourhood to neighbourhood, from Malir Tanki, Malir City, Liaqat Market, Jinnah Square and Model Colony, of all ages and classes, looked up to him for spiritual guidance. There were some special friends: a street vendor called Ahsan, a radio mechanic at Malir Tanki, and a 'master sahib', a teacher of Islamic Studies, in Kulsum Bai Valika School at the airport, who Waheed Mammu visited quite regularly. And there was one very special person the Maulana saw every day: a roaming hermit called Khalil of Malir Tanki Market, who wore or ate very little and did not mind what or when he ate or wore.

Thus I discovered something that frankly I should have been able to see all along; if only I had the ability to see. Now it was obvious that Waheed Mammu was a mystic and belonged to a mystical group. The surprising element was that he was highly respected and venerated by his followers, and that he was actually living the life of a hermit. But that did not explain his vanishing trick. Nani Jaan, however, was satisfied with the discovery. 'He has been appropriated by God,' she declared. A year later, in 1981, she decided to go for a pilgrimage to Mecca. Waheed Mammu, who nourished a burning desire for *hajj*, was eager to accompany her. He tried his utmost to convince Nani Jaan to take him along, as she was required to be accompanied by a close male family member, and also because he did not want to be without her. But she was adamant on going alone. On the appointed day, everyone went to see grandma off. She was going by ship and the entire extended family gathered at Jetty 23 of the port of Karachi. Just before embarking, she declared, 'I am sure that darn son of mine is already on the ship.' He was. At her insistence, the ship was thoroughly searched and he was forcefully removed.

After Nani Jaan returned from *hajj*, Waheed Mammu began to spend considerable time at the shrine of a local saint, Pir Bokhari. This was a cause for concern, because the area around the shrine had a notorious reputation; abductions and gun battles between police and gangs were a common occurrence. He visited Nani Jaan reguarly, often bringing a portion of the food offering that was made at the shrine for his mother. He always carried with him a plastic bag containing spare clothes and tooth powder, and some sweetmeats. She hated the sight of his plastic bag and refused to eat his food. He would try and put some sweetmeat in her mouth—which she would eventually accept. The ritual repeated itself on a daily basis.

Then, in January 1994, Nani Jaan died. She was 95, give or take a few years, and did housework every day of her life. On the day before her death, she cleaned the house, helped the family prepare the dinner and died peacefully during the night. Her death had a profound effect on Waheed Mammu; although he controlled himself outwardly, his smile and playfulness disappeared, and he changed his routine. He visited her grave twice a day: he would clean and wash it, leave flowers, and recite the Qur'an. His followers built a little enclave around the grave, and placed a carved marble stone at the head. The epitaph read 'Mother of brother Waheed'.

Waheed Mammu drifted away from the family after Nani Jaan's death. His visits became rare—although he kept in touch by telephone. His favourite family members, like Gudu, often received several calls a day. He also began to use the English word 'vanish': whenever he came across a member of the family, or was spotted by them in the neighbourhood, he would loudly utter 'vanish' and then disappear. Family elders became concerned both about the increasing distance between him and his relatives, as well as his health, which was clearly deteriorating. So another plan was devised to bring Waheed Mammu back. Relatives in London decided to send the elders in Karachi for pilgrimage to Mecca. The party of eight included Waheed Mammu and two younger men, Gudu and his younger brother, Guda, to look after the seniors. We thought that Waheed Mammu, with his deep desire to visit the holy land, would be pleased and eager to go. We also assumed that he did not have a passport, so Gudu acquired a passport for him. It appeared that Waheed Mammu was ready for the journey. But he failed to turn up on the day when all intending pilgrims had to report to the Pilgrim Centre for last minute document-checking. Indeed, he could not be found anywhere. Search parties were sent to the shrine of Pir Bukhari and other places we knew he frequented. His followers informed the family that in fact he was not even in Karachi. Everyone was furious and confused. Reluctantly, the party went without him.

I was particularly angry and puzzled. Why would Waheed Mammu not go to Mecca, when he desired nothing else in this life more than to perform the *hajj*? We discovered soon afterwards that Waheed Mammu had actually been to Mecca to perform the *umra*, or lesser pilgrimage. A year after Nani Jaan went on *hajj* without him, his followers, led by street vendor Ahsan, financed a trip for him and his devotees, to Mecca. But there was something more, and that, I had to wait till a short visit to Karachi in 1997 to discover.

Waheed Mammu turned up literally a few minutes after I reached Model Colony. I was overjoyed to discover that he had not lost his fondness for me. He embraced me; it was not so much of a warm embrace as a very tight squeeze. He looked pale, and was clearly not well.

'Are you all right?' I asked.

'Oh,' he replied, 'I have got high blood pressure. You know it runs in the family.'

We sat on the *charpoy* on the veranda, under the papaya tree, and chatted.

'Have you given any money to the poor today?' he asked.

I knew there was only one answer to this question. I took out a hundred rupee note from my pocket and handed to him. We got up and walked outside. There was a beggar passing by and Waheed Mammu signalled for him to come over. As Waheed Mammu was handing the money to him, I grabbed his wrist.

'This man,' I inquired, 'is not just any old beggar is he?'

Waheed Mammu gave me one of his special smiles, the expression he used when he appeared to be speechless. I half expected him to say 'vanish'. He didn't.

'No,' he said.

'In fact,' I said with a big grin on my face, 'he is the same beggar you have been giving my alms to for the past 25 years!'

'He is one of my followers.'

I noticed that there were two men standing not too far from the door, one of them was leaning on a motor cycle. I walked over to the man with the motor cycle.

'Are you waiting for the Maulana?' I asked.

'Yes', he replied.

'You do not have to wait because he will be a long time,' I said.

'I'll wait for as long as it takes,' he replied. 'I am on duty for him.'

'What do you mean?' I asked.

'I am on duty to escort the Maulana anywhere he wishes till 9 p.m. After that someone else takes over,' he replied.

'How many of you are on duty?'

'Two for conveyance purposes,' he replied. 'There are six more with other duties.'

He pointed to various people who were hanging around the street.

'What other duties?' I asked.

'Well,' the motor cycle man replied, 'we have to deliver money to widows, arrange funerals for families who cannot undertake the task themselves, attend to accident victims... That sort of duties.'

'And all eight of you move together as one,' I inquired.

'No, no,' said the man. 'There are eight people here with specific duties. But there are many more.'

'How many?'

'Oh I don't know,' he said. He started looking around and counting; he gave up after thirty. 'All of us,' said the man with the motorcycle, 'we move as a *tolly*.'

'As a gathering,' I murmured to myself.

I looked back at Waheed Mammu; he was still standing there, the same special smile on his face. 'Vanish,' he said.

'Vanish,' I said, as I moved out of the way of the motorcycle.

The mystery of Waheed Mammu had finally been resolved. He was a part of an invisible network of mystics and social workers that moved through the city as one. Indeed, he never actually existed on his own—as an individual. He was always surrounded by members of his network, each ever ready to do whatever was necessary. The 'strangers' he met on the streets were in fact not strangers are all—they were fellow travellers. When we saw him sitting on the back of a motorbike, waving to us, he was not hitching a ride from a stranger—but one of his 'on duty' followers was taking him to his next task. During our visit to Zahida *khala* in Maripur, when the rickshaw-wallah would only take two passengers and we had to leave him behind, he was taken there by one of his 'on duty' disciples, on the only vehicle that can negotiate the traffic of Karachi better than a rickshaw: a moped. One of them bought milk from the market while another made the tea! When we left him locked up in the windowless room in Nani Jaan's house, and went to take the train to Bhawalnagar, he was immediately let out by his followers, who also helped him identify the right couch for the journey—indeed, his entire invisible network travelled with us to Bhawalnagar. Waheed Mammu did not want to go on *hajj* because that meant going to Mecca as an *individual*, without his network. His followers, Ahsan, the street vendor, and 'Master Sahib', the Islamic studies teacher, later told us that they tried to make preparations for a group of his disciples to accompany him, but there just wasn't enough time to make the appropriate arrangements. When Waheed Mammu 'vanished', he vanished to perform an urgent social task. His network, we learned, was often amongst the first to attend to the dead and wounded after a horrendous road accident, which are a common enough sight in Karachi. His network looked after countless widows, orphans and handicapped people; organised the burial of the homeless; transported the sick and infirm to the hospital; and helped the poor and the needy in countless other ways. The network wasn't invisible—but it took over quarter of a century for me to actually see it. By all accounts, Karachi and other Pakistani cities have numerous other such networks.

That was the last time I saw Waheed Mammu. He did make a number of other trips to the family house—particularly when my mother came for a visit from London. After Nani Jaan's death, he become particularly close to Mumsey, the only person he now looked up to. He would always be accompanied by his network: two members would stay outside the door, often for hours, till he came out to be taken to his next destination. During this period, Waheed Mammu became preoccupied with looking after the roaming hermit Khalil. There was a strong spiritual bond between the two; even though Khalil was much older, it was difficult to say which was the Master and which the Disciple. I never actually saw the two together. But the family members who did talk about 'a strong spiritual presence created by two comets merging into one', of 'unconditional love and devotion' between the two, and being 'shaken and affected' by seeing the two together. It is hardly surprising, then, that Khalil's death, in May 2004, left Waheed Mammu in total paralysis.

In the early morning of Wednesday 14 July 2004—exactly 39 days after the death of Khalil—Gudu received a telephone call. It was a senior member of Waheed Mammu's network. Baba had collapsed, he said, and has been taken to the Accident and Emergency Unit of Karachi's Jinnah Hospital. When Gudu and other members of the family arrived at the hospital, they found him lying unconscious on a bed 'with all sorts of pipes attached to his body'. He had been diagnosed with a brain haemorrhage and very high blood pressure. The doctors had declared that he had zero chance of survival. While Ward 6, and the area around it, was full of Waheed Mammu's followers, they stood at a respectable distance, allowing the family some privacy with him. Only Ahsan the street vendor joined the family. He told Gudu: 'Last night, Baba instructed us to arrange a big reception, with his favourite dishes. Then he oversaw the table being properly laid and ate to his heart's content. On reaching his usual abode in the shrine he felt sick, vomited twice and fainted. We immediately brought him to the hospital. Others informed Baba's relatives on whatever phone numbers we could get from his little blue notebook.'

Family members took turns sitting beside Waheed Mammu's bed. The doctors gave him another check-up; still no change in his condition. Then a string of women started arriving, all respectfully veiled: a group of them stood beside the bed for a few moments, and then moved on, their place taken by another group. Around three o'clock, the doctors announced that Waheed Mammu had died. His body was driven in an ambulance to Model Colony. According to the expressed wishes of his mystical network, he was laid to rest next to his friend Khaleel, amid moving scenes of adulation and admiration on the part of his religious followers, male as well as female, in a cemetery near Karachi Airport. His small bag, containing one pair of *kurta-pajama*, tooth powder and a blue notebook—his entire worldly possessions—were placed by his grave side. Some of Waheed Mammu's followers wanted to build a small mausoleum over his grave, but the family overruled their suggestion.

On my next visit to Karachi, I discovered that Waheed Mammu's grave, in the Model Colony Cemetery (New), had actually been turned into a mausoleum. It took a while for Gudu and his son to lead the expedition to the exact spot. When we arrived, what we found is a small but impressive building, its ceiling decorated with elaborate motifs and calligraphy in the style of Persian miniature paintings. There are two graves inside; outside a sign in Urdu declares it is the tomb of 'Hazrat Baba Khalil Shah Qalandari' and 'Hazrat Baba Waheed Ahmad Khan Qalandari'. The full honorifics of their titles signify that both were Sufi mystics in good standing, makers of outstanding contributions to general humanity and full measure of humaneness. Two members of his network are constantly 'on duty', tending the grave, laying flowers, cleaning the mausoleum. A senior member is always present to recount the details of Khalil Tanki and Waheed Mammu's biographies. There is a constant flow of old and new followers who come to pray for his salvation and listen to the stories of his life.

In death, as in life, Waheed Mammu continues to teach that there is more than one way to travel through the complexities of being human. Resolving the enigma that was my Waheed Mammu was the work of decades. As I stood in his mausoleum to comprehend his story, I had a deeper understanding of how and why I need to acknowledge my own Pakistani roots. For truly, he turned out to be a person of Pakistani origins.

REFERENCES

1. A Person of Pakistani Origins

Carol Ann Duffy's poem 'Birmingham for Tariq Jahan' was published in *The Guardian* of 12 August 2011. The messages promoted in Pakistani history textbooks are described in K. K. Aziz's *The Murder of History: A Critique of History Textbooks Used in Pakistan* (Vanguard, Lahore, 2004), pp. 187–205.

My documentary 'Battle for Islam' was broadcast on BBC 2, 12 September 2005, 21.00–22:30.

The books cited include: *Islamic Futures: The Shape of Ideas to Come* (Mansell, London, 1985); *Why Do People Hate America* (Icon Books, London; Disinformation Books, New York, 2012); *Desperately Seeking Paradise: Journey of a Sceptical Muslim* (Granta, London, 2004) and *Balti Britain: A Provocative Journey Through Asian Britain* (Granta, London, 2008). The Saadat Hassan Manto lecture, 'Coming Home: Sex, Lies and all the '!'s in India', was published in Futures, 29: 10 (1997), pp. 891–908, and reprinted in *How Do You Know? Reading Ziauddin Sardar on Islam, Science and Cultural Relations*, edited by Ehsan Masood, (Pluto, London, 2006).

2. Ibn Safi, BA

This essay was first published in *Critical Muslim 4: Pakistan* (Hurst, London, 2012).

A number of Ibn-e-Safi novels have been translated in English; mostly recently *The House of Fear*, translated by Bilal Tanweer and *The*

227

REFERENCES

Dangerous Man, translated by Taimoor Shahid (both Random House India, 2009 and 2011). But no translation can do justice to ibn-e-Safi's playful language, full of innuendos and puns. He is best read in original Urdu, and a number of his novels are available for free downloads from a host of sites, such as http://imranseries.urdunovels.org/category/imran-series-by-ibne-safi/ and http://freeurdubooks4u.blogspot.co.uk/2011/03/ibn-safi-jasoosi-dunya-novels-complete.html

The ibn-e-Safi website (http://www.ibnesafi.info/), clearly a labour of love, contains all one needs to know about Ibn-e-Safi. For more on adventures of Hakim Sahib, see *Ziauddin Sardar, Balti Britain* (Granta, 2008).

3. Two Books and an Auntie

This article first appeared in *Asia Literary Review* (Spring 2008), pp. 129–142; and was republished in *Critical Muslim 21: Relations* (Hurst, London, 2017). Bihishti Zewari is translated by Barbara Daly Metcalf as *Perfecting Women* (University of California Press, reprint edition, 1992). Mirat ul-Arus is translated by G E. Ward as *Brides Mirror: A Tale of Life in Delhi A 100 Years Ago* (Orient Longman, Delhi, 2004).

4. Dilip Kumar Made Me Do It

First published as Chapter 2 of Ashis Nandy (ed.), *A Secret History our Desires: Innocence, Culpability and Indian Popular Cinema*, (London, Zed Press, 1999).

The quote from Naushad is from an interview for the documentary series 'Peacock Screen'; the four episodes of the series were broadcast on Channel 4 during December/January 1991. The special edition of 'Eastern Eye' on Amitabh Bachchan was broadcast on Channel 4 on 12 July 1983. My interview with Dilip Kumar appeared in the last edition of the first series of 'Eastern Eye' broadcast on Channel 4 on 23 August 1993. The sections broadcast focused on Dilip Kumar's acting career and his films. All the quotations for this article are from an extended interview which was not recorded by broadcast.

The quotation from Kishore Valicha is from *The Moving Image: A Study of Indian Cinema* (Orient Longman, Bombay, 1988), p. 49; the Satyajit Ray quote is from *Our Films, Their Films* (Orient Longman, Bombay,

REFERENCES

1976), from the essay entitled, 'An Indian New Wave', p. 82; the Satish Bahadur quote is from 'The Context of Indian Film Culture' in *Film Appreciation Study Material* (series 2, National Film Archive of India, 1978); quoted by Valicha, op cit., p. 36; and the Michael Medved quote is from *Hollywood vs America* (HarperCollins, London, 1993. Extracts from the book appeared in the Sunday Times on 7, 14, 21 and 28 February and 7 March 1993.

For an analysis of the films of Arnold Schwarzenegger see Ziauddin Sardar, 'Total Recall: Aliens, Others and Amnesia in Postmodernism', Futures, 23: 2 (March 1991), pp. 189–203 and 'Terminator 2: Modernity, Postmodernity and Judgement Day', *Futures*, 25: 5, pp. 493–506 (June 1992).

5. Love, Death and Urdu Poetry

I have benefited from T. Grahame Baily, *A History of Urdu Literature* (Lahore, 1932); Gopi Chand Narang, *Urdu Language and Literature: Critical Perspectives* (Vanguard, Lahore, 1991); David Matthews, *An Anthology of Urdu Verse in English* (OUP, Bombay, 1995); Mahmood Jamal, *The Penguin Book of Modern Urdu Poetry* (London, 1986); *Faiz: Fifty Poems*, compiled and translated by Mahmood Jamal (OUP, Karachi); Raza Mir, *The Taste of Words* (Penguin, Delhi, 2014); and Salil Kuldip, *Great Urdu Ghazals* (Hind Pocket Books, 2011). On the mythology of Insha ji utto, see Ali Raj, 'Asad Amanat /Ali Khan and the Myth of the Cursed Ghazal', *The Express Tribune*, 7 April 2016; and Nadeem Paracha, 'The Cursed Song', *Dawn*, 1 November 2015.

The *NFT/Guardian* interview with Shashi Kapoor was on 7 November 1993.

ACKNOWLEDGEMENTS

Thanks are due to my friend and serial collaborator, Merryl Wyn Davies, a fan of Dilip Kumar and lover of Urdu poetry, for her advice and encouragements. And to Scott Jordan for his comments and support.